LEW

The Life and Times of the Author of *Ben Hur*

Michael F. Fox

SUNBURY
P R E S S ®
Mechanicsburg, PA USA

Published by Sunbury Press, Inc.
Mechanicsburg, PA USA

SUNBURY
PRESS
www.sunburypress.com

For information about special discounts for bulk purchases, please contact Sunbury Press Orders Dept. at (855) 338-8359 or orders@sunburypress.com.

To request one of our authors for speaking engagements or book signings, please contact Sunbury Press Publicity Dept. at publicity@sunburypress.com.

FIRST SUNBURY PRESS EDITION: February 2024

Set in Adobe Garamond Pro | Interior design by Crystal Devine | Cover by Lawrence Knorr | Edited by Sarah Illick.

Publisher's Cataloging-in-Publication Data
Names: Fox, Michael E., author.
Title: LEW : the life and times of the author of Ben Hur / Michael E. Fox.
Description: First trade paperback edition. | Mechanicsburg, PA : Sunbury Press, 2024.
Summary: *LEW, The Life and Times of the Author of Ben Hur*, is a broad and rich historical biography of a great American author who is little known or remembered today. Lew Wallace, a fascinating and multitalented historical figure, has consistently been overlooked and lost in academia, articles, and books. When he is discussed, he is often misrepresented and misunderstood. This book addresses the errors and misconceptions.
Identifiers: ISBN : 979-8-88819-191-0 (paperback) | ISBN : 979-8-88819-192-7 (ePub).
Subjects: HISTORY / United States / 19th Century | BIOGRAPHY & AUTOBIOGRAPHY / Historical | RELIGION / History.

Product of the United States of America
0 1 1 2 3 5 8 13 21 34 55

For the Love of Books!

CONTENTS

Introduction

The novel *Ben Hur, A Tale of the Christ*, was published in 1880 and two years later became a best seller and one of the most successful books of all time. An estimated fifty million copies have been sold worldwide, and it continues to be printed and distributed 140 years later. It has been translated into at least twenty languages, including Arabic, Portuguese, Thai, and Hebrew. It has never been out of print and is often touted as the most religiously significant book of the nineteenth century, second only to the Bible. It was blessed by Pope Leo XIII (1878–1903) as the first novel ever to receive such an honor. It has been heralded as a story that has brought many people to their feet to cheer and many others to their knees to pray. It remained the top-selling novel until Margaret Mitchel's *Gone with the Wind* in 1936, a period of fifty-four years.

There was a major Broadway play adapted in 1899. A short silent film was released in 1907—three major motion pictures were produced in 1925, 1959, and 2016. The 1959 version, starring Charlton Heston, won eleven Academy Awards and was viewed by millions. It is considered one of the greatest films of all time. In 1960, *Ben Hur* became the number-one selling book again. An animated film version, narrated by Charlton Heston, was released on children's television in 2003 and a television miniseries in 2010. Yet, most of the time, when I ask people if they know the author's name, I get a blank stare. Famous authors and books published around the same era, such as *Uncle Tom's Cabin*, *Huckleberry Finn*, and *Gone with the Wind*, people usually know. However, *Ben Hur* has outsold all those books and was adapted to other significant forms of entertainment at least seven times over 120 years. The author's name is Lew Wallace, and in his autobiography, Lew claims to have written seven parts of *Ben Hur* in Crawfordsville, Indiana, and the eighth and final part in Santa Fé, New Mexico, while serving as territorial governor.

My father moved our family to Crawfordsville when I was five. It was the summer of 1959. Our new town of 10,000 inhabitants was booming, and the people were abuzz over a newly released blockbuster film based on a book primarily written there. As a family, we went to see it at "The Strand," an ornate, renovated, traditional theater made into a movie house. It was a captivating environment, with large retractable crimson curtains highlighted by footlights covering the movie screen. Low-intensity purple lights shined on draped private balconies and alcoves, and an ornate illuminated domed ceiling hovered above. The remainder of the room was dark except for the aisle lighting. It was my first time in an indoor movie theater, and I was excited. Finally, the drapes parted, and the movie began, transporting the audience to an ancient time and place in technicolor. *Ben Hur* was mesmerizing for the next three hours and thirty minutes, and I became a dedicated lifetime movie fan.

Only seven years later and barely twelve, I started working at the Green Street Barber Shop, shining shoes and cleaning up hair, cigarette butts, ashes, and tobacco juice. The shop had four cutting chairs, and it's where the best yarn was spun, and I eavesdropped on every story I could. One of the barbers was Alexander "Homer" Bonnell. He was a Spanish-American War veteran, still cutting hair in his mid-eighties. He grew up just around the corner from Lew Wallace's home and study during Wallace's lifetime. Homer had always lived in the same house, continued to walk back and forth to work each day, rain or shine, and still worked on his feet eight hours, five days a week. I struck a friendship with him and traded free shines for haircuts. He was a little unsteady of hand by then, so his shaves with the straight razor around my ears and down the neck sometimes left me slightly wounded. But I willingly gave a little of my blood to sit in his chair as he plied his trade, chewed, spit, and sometimes actually spoke. Just being around Homer was a joy and treasure. He was a true gentleman, a remnant of a more civilized time.

He was exceedingly polite and always respectful, and I never remember hearing him raise his voice, swear, or utter a cross word.

Even when some unruly locals wandered in with a "snoot full" after an early afternoon at the local bars, Homer stared at them with a look that could cower a bull. It was never a mean look, just disarming. Everyone knew Homer, and they showed him the respect he deserved. One day, he shared a story from 1898 when Lew Wallace sat down with him and fellow volunteers to speak about going to war with Spain. Wallace shared his raw and unfettered war experiences. There was a look in his eyes as he spoke to each recruit, and Homer said he would never forget: an intense black that seemed to penetrate Homer's brain. No doubt everyone heard the message, and although eloquently given, it was unnerving. Only eighteen years old, Homer subsequently proceeded to war. Listening to Homer tell those occasional stories made me feel like I had a better-than-average image of Lew Wallace. Maybe I did, or perhaps I didn't, but spending time with someone like Homer got me as close as I could ever get.

Wallace was known as "Lew" to his friends and neighbors. He could have been addressed as counselor, major general, governor, minister, or the great author Lew Wallace. I interacted with many Crawfordsville elderly while working at the Ben Hur Nursing Home through college (the home is a remnant of Ben Hur Life Insurance Company). I unclogged their plumbing, repaired and painted their walls, fixed their beds, fans, and radios, and even filled Mrs. Peacock's bird feeder as needed. Some residents were well into their nineties, still mentally sharp. I soaked up their stories and wisdom. A few had known Lew and his family during his retirement years. The person their stories created in my mind was a socially elevated, decidedly eccentric man but friendly and approachable. I learned Lew's close friends and family lamented his lack of self-promotion, which they felt robbed him of greater fame and fortune. It is speculated this perceived reluctance was rooted in caution from past adverse events in his life. If these theories are true, they explain Lew being a slightly obscure, albeit significant historical figure.

Lew's most famous book stirred a powerful Christian resurgence, while the man remains an enigma in his religious beliefs. He was never an official member of any church or denomination and didn't believe he was a suitable communicant. The main character and hero in *Ben Hur*, who many believe is a partial literary version of Lew Wallace, is a Jewish prince from Judea who eventually converts to Christianity. His subsequent book, *The Boyhood of Christ*, is a more traditional view of Christianity. But one of his later books, *The Prince of India: Or, Why Constantinople Fell*, is about a legendary wandering Jew in the guise of a prince of India who contributed to the city's downfall and empire by aiding and advising the Turkish Sultan Mehmed II. Each book Lew published seemed to bring forth a different author, one as equally complex as the other.

Lew's life is a fascinating and confusing historical study. He was proud, highly intelligent, well-read, and predominantly self-educated. His values were uncompromising, and his youthful arrogance and ambition sometimes did not serve him well. Lew became embroiled in several controversies, leaving a perplexing legacy. Many of his traits were the foundation from which he achieved great personal success while also rendering him easy prey to others lacking his tenets. His drive to achieve fame and fortune worked against him, implicating him in alleged lapses of judgment and rendering him a scapegoat. Some unscrupulous characters took advantage of Lew's sense of duty to insert him into legal and political prosecutions doomed to controversy, hoping to shelter themselves from potential social and political backlash. Regardless of the controversies, it's essential to remember between 1860 and 1890, when someone in the United States government needed a person of confidence, ability, and integrity to handle a complex or controversial situation, Lew Wallace was often on their list.

Lew experienced significant tragedies before he was eight. Over four years during the Civil War, he was labeled a brilliant field commander, an inept general, a competent administrator, and then a savior of the nation's capital at age thirty-seven. He became a signatory, protagonist, or advocate for three of the most controversial executions in the history of the United States, occurring between 1865 and 1881. All three were executed for alleged crimes during a historical or quasi-historical war. These high-profile conflicts and controversies relentlessly resurfaced and haunted Lew until his death. They remain unearthed in articles, books, television programs, miniseries, and movies. The same events occurring in Lew's life continue to play out in contemporary affairs. History does indeed repeat itself, and this book highlights some of these present-day situations.

I've been listening, reading, and researching history for years, but I hadn't intended to publish a book. On the contrary, I'm happily retired from what Lew considered the most detestable of all professions: the practice of law. Somewhere along my journey into retirement, I felt the need to start researching and writing for reasons that still escape me. Maybe my initial motivation was to leave a legacy related to my hometown. I honestly have no idea, but I began to piece together fragmented incidents and accomplishments from a man's life that screamed for collective recognition. It certainly wasn't my life. It was the life of someone I'd never met. Growing up in Crawfordsville and always interested in local history, I became aware of Lew Wallace's many accomplishments and controversies. They were always expressed in singularity, and each one to me was unremarkable. One day, while brainstorming, I combined all the fragments, piecing together all the significant historical moments before and during Lew's lifetime, and the resulting collage was extraordinary. So, I wrote for months and collected my findings in this book.

It's not an arduous, detailed biography and not intended to be one. This book is as much a sketch of a tumultuous yet inspirational period in American history as it is of Lew's life and how it all culminated into a significant piece of nineteenth-century literature. However, we also know free will, choices, and life experiences affect and change people. Many have writing talent, but few can write highly successful novels like *Ben Hur*. By the end, the reader should have an enhanced appreciation of Lew as a writer and a man. He is unique in a list of other significant American authors. As a bonus, my readings and research uncovered some interesting claims and coincidental happenings that are not well-known. These items may trigger legitimate questions in readers' minds concerning the validity of previously accepted historical facts.

—MICHAEL E. FOX

PART 1

From a Political Cradle

Youth is but the painted shell within which, continually growing, lives that wondrous thing the spirit of a man, biding its moment of apparition, earlier in some than in others.

—LEW WALLACE, *BEN HUR: A TALE OF CHRIST*[1]

---

1. Goodreads, "Lew Wallace Quotes," accessed October 23, 2023, https://www.goodreads.com/quotes/570224-youth-is-but-the-painted-shell-within-which-continually-growing.

Brookville

Sometime in 1817, a man named Andrew Wallace—a storekeeper in Carlisle, Pennsylvania, a surveyor in Troy, Ohio, and then a publisher in Cincinnati—emigrated with his family of eight children to a small town in southeast Indiana named Brookville and began operating a tavern. During the War of 1812, Andrew Wallace was a quartermaster and confidant of American General William Henry Harrison. Due to his relationship with Harrison, he obtained an appointment for his eldest son, David, to the military academy at West Point.

After graduating from West Point, David Wallace taught mathematics for one year at the academy, then resigned his commission and returned to his hometown of Brookville. He studied law and, in 1823, began his practice in the offices of John Test. In 1824, he married Esther French Test, John Test's daughter. Andrew Wallace died in Brookville in 1826. Lewis "Lew" Wallace, David Wallace's second of four sons, was born on April 10, 1827, so Lew never knew his paternal grandfather. But Andrew, having been a good friend of General Harrison, gave the Wallace family strong political connections. Harrison eventually became the ninth president of the United States but died thirty-one days later of pneumonia, the shortest period in office of any US president.[1]

John Test served in the United States Congress from 1823 to 1827 and was again elected to Congress in 1829 as an anti-Jackson candidate

---

1. The White House, "William Henry Harrison, The 9th President of the United States," accessed December 30, 2023, https://www.whitehouse.gov/about-the-white-house/presidents/william-henry-harrison/.

and served until 1831.² Therefore, Lew's family political connections on his maternal side were also significant. Around 1832, John Test experienced a difficult financial period, thought to have occurred through some speculative ventures, and eventually moved to Mobile, Alabama, where he started a new law practice.³ In early 1832, when Lew was barely five, David Wallace moved his young family from Brookville to Covington, Indiana, 160 miles northwest of Brookville. David became a silent partner with a brother living in Covington who started a merchandising enterprise. David moved his family under the primary premise of assisting his brother in his new business affairs. At the same time, many speculated he was distancing himself from his father-in-law's societal descension, as he had his own political aspirations. All four of David and Esther Wallace's boys born in Brookville had the distinguishing feature of black eyes.⁴

Covington, located in west-central Indiana, is approximately thirty miles west of Crawfordsville near the Illinois border. The town is situated on the banks of the Wabash River, a major transportation waterway. The family's trip from Brookville to Covington was by animal-drawn carriage, requiring them to pass through Indianapolis. A carriage could average twenty-five to thirty miles daily if it moved at a steady pace between feeding, watering, occasional blows, overnight rest, and possible blacksmith, harness repair, or farrier service.⁵ Often, family members walked alongside the animals to ease their burden. In 1832, the distance between larger towns with sufficient traveler lodging and service amenities was about one day's travel. Similar distancing between larger towns exists today. To travel 160 miles with a young family, David Wallace had to estimate a minimum of seven days over muddy or dusty roads before arriving in Covington. It was an arduous trip for a young family of six, and a great tragedy befell them during the journey when Lew and his

2. Biographical Directory of the United States Congress, "John Test 1781–1849," accessed December 30, 2023, https://bioguide.congress.gov/search/bio/T000138.

3. In addition to being a congressman and lawyer, John Test owned a grist mill in Brookville, producing dry goods.

4. Lew Wallace, *An Autobiography, Vol 1*, (Forgotten Books 2015), 8 : eyeXam Silicon Valley, accessed December 30, 2023, https:eyeexam.com/6-rare-unique-eye-colors/. Black eyes do not exist. It is a rare phenomenon where the eyes only appear black due to abundant melanin. Melanin is a substance in the body that produces pigmentation. The more melanin, the darker the eyes, but they never reach total black. However, without sufficient light projected on the eyes, it is difficult to delineate the pupil from the iris, and the eye appears black.

5. A farrier is a person who does hoof trimming and shoeing. A harness maker would make and repair harnesses, and a blacksmith would repair wagons, wheels, brakes, and axils. Many times, the town blacksmith could provide all three services. A "blow" is jargon for letting a horse stop, rest, catch its breath, and regain stamina.

younger brother John contracted scarlet fever. The family was forced to pause their trip and seek medical care for the boys in Indianapolis.

Three things left a lasting impression on five-year-old Lew while in Indianapolis: His brother John died from the fever, followed by the flow of heartbroken tears from his mother's dark brown eyes and the awful scalding draughts of saffron tea, which he was relentlessly forced to drink. Lew would write in his autobiography many years later that the Arabs referred to the first five years of a person's life as the "days of ignorance," but by five, Lew had already experienced hard lessons concerning long-distance travel, sickness, the fragility of life, and the emotional pain borne by a family when a loved one is lost.[6] His days of ignorance reached a tragic and distressing end, for these early experiences most certainly hardened and prepared him for future tragedies as his life and professional career progressed.

---

6. Wallace, *An Autobiography*, (Forgotten Books 2015), 8.

Covington

When young Lew arrived in Covington, he observed four posts and the scaffolding of gallows used to hang a man for murder. It lurked low in the darkness of trees in a slight hollow carved out by the Wabash River overflow. The structure was pointed out by someone Lew described as an "ignorant servant girl" who purportedly witnessed the hanging. She explained the event in great detail; first, she recounted the crowd of people watching. Second, she described the rope and knot procured from a "special source" in Kentucky, with the strategic location of the knot directly behind the man's left ear. Third, how the sheriff stifled the man with a hood when he attempted to proclaim his innocence. Fourth, the loud bang of the trap door and the chilling silence that fell over the crowd as the victim convulsed. Fifth, when the doctor checked for a pulse and pronounced the victim dead. Finally, the body's removal as a line gathered for a piece of the rope as a souvenir.[1]

Lew's narrator may have seemed ignorant, but she left little to the imagination and burned lasting imagery into her young listener's brain.

After a thorough education in public hangings, Lew turned his attention to the river bordering Covington. Rivers and other waterways remained a constant source of attraction, leisure, and tragedy throughout his life. In 1832, the Wabash River had its headwaters in far western Ohio and then meandered through Indiana for over 500 miles. It remains the largest northern tributary of the Ohio River and the third-largest tributary

---

1. Ibid., 12.

behind the Cumberland and Tennessee Rivers, and its watershed drains most of Indiana. It decidedly turns south at Covington and becomes the border between Illinois and Indiana at approximately mile 300 from its headwaters. Some 200 winding miles later, it joins the Ohio. In 1832, from Covington to the Ohio, the Wabash remained consistently deep and wide enough to support large water transport vessels of the day carrying various finished goods and commodities.

Shortly after his sixth birthday, Lew befriended a man named Nebeker, who ran a ferry service across the river. Nebeker let Lew hang out with him any day Lew would show up and often shared his lunch and dinner with the boy. Lew, in turn, assisted Nebeker in tending his ferry lines while also spending hours catching minnows and staring into the river dangling precariously over the ferry's gunnels.[2] Intently watching the movement of the murky waters, Lew experienced exhilaration and dark magnetism. He was so enamored with these activities that he blamed the coaxing power of the river for contributing to his habit of truancy, which lasted throughout his school years. Over seventy years later, Lew proclaimed he had seen the Danube, the Rhine, and the Nile, and none had impressed nor moved him like the Wabash.[3]

In 1897, a traveling Vaudeville comedian and actor named Paul Dresser wrote a song called "On the Banks of the Wabash, Far Away." In the lyrics, the writer reminisces about his childhood living along the Wabash in Terre Haute, Indiana. The song was first published and sold in sheet music and quickly became one of the best-selling songs of the nineteenth century. It is estimated over one million copies were sold at a total revenue of $100,000, which were astronomical numbers for sheet music in those days. The song would later be audio-recorded numerous times and was one of the first known phonograph cylinder releases. Indiana made it their state song in 1913, and Bing Crosby recorded it on vinyl as late as 1959. It has inspired numerous lyrical versions, including an anti-war song in 1898 and even a Swedish version that was a number-one hit.

---

2. A gunnel is a nautical term phonetically derived from gunwales, meaning the point where the top of the sides of a floating vessel is connected to its deck. Any structure above that connection point is known as a "bulwark" that helps prevent people and cargo from going overboard. However, most river ferries in 1832 were relatively flat vessels and did not have substantial bulwarks.

3. Wallace, *An Autobiography,* Vol. 1, 10.

Interestingly, the height of the song's influence coincided with the continuing success of the then-current best-selling novel *Ben Hur*. However, the crowning attestation to the popularity of the music was an incident in June of 1900 at the Coney Island Arena in New York. Terry McGovern and Tommy White were in the middle of a featherweight title fight's first round when all the lights in the arena failed. The crowd panicked, and a quick-thinking ring announcer started whistling the tune to the popular Indiana song, at which point the group relaxed and sang the verses until the lights were repaired and the fight could continue.[4]

---

4. Alchetron, "Terry McGovern (boxer)," accessed January 12, 2024, https://alchetron.com/Terry-McGovern-(boxer): In the infamous "lights out match" at the Coney Island Arena, Terry McGovern knocked Tommy White's lights out in a third round KO and retained his featherweight title. White, born in Fox Lake, IL, and fighting out of Chicago had the odd boxing alias of "Board of Trade Pet." Born and fighting out of Brooklyn, NY, McGovern was known as "Terrible Terry."

School Days

Lew's first encounter with school created more terror and trauma than for most six-year-old boys. His schoolmaster was a man who had a penchant for giving impactful and memorable corporal punishment. Lew recalled him focusing on back-flogging and appeared to treat it as a part of his professional skill set. The schoolmaster hung rods of various lengths and gauges in the classroom to fit the age and size of the transgressor, as well as the severity of the transgression. From Lew's memory, his teacher singled out truancy as a felonious act of the highest aggravation. Therefore, since Lew had developed it as a self-professed practice, his posterior remained in constant inflammation throughout his initial school year.

As Lew's life progressed, he did not respond well to heavy-handed management methods. His father also used a rod, so one could speculate the schoolmaster and Lew's father left a lasting impression on the young boy that transcended the physical. Despite constant floggings, Lew never modified his behavior for long. On the other hand, public scrutiny, criticism, and embarrassment affected him profoundly and altered his conduct. Lew credited his mother and older brother for teaching him the alphabet and how to spell, and he discovered he had a better-than-average talent for drawing faces and figures than his peers while sketching during class time.

After a significant event in the region, Lew developed an interest in military conflict and utilized his newly discovered talents to draw imaginary battlefields. He crowded the fictional landscapes with numerous combatants; the more, the merrier.

Black Hawk War

The Black Hawk War got its name from a one-eyed Sauk Indian war chief named Black Hawk. The war began after the chief led a group of Sauks, Meskwakis, and Kickapoos, collectively known then as the British Band, east across the Mississippi River from Iowa Indian country into Illinois in the spring of 1832. Although the Band's true intentions were never fully understood, they might have simply been trying to resettle lands the government claimed they sold in the disputed 1804 Treaty of St. Louis. Native leaders negotiated the treaty with then-territorial Governor William Henry Harrison. The United States claimed the Sauk and Meskwakis sold all their land east of the Mississippi for $2,200 in goods and annual payments of $1,000, also in goods—a suspiciously paltry sum even for that time when considering the size of the territory.[1]

The history of events and situations leading up to and during the war is complex. Many historians speculate the 1804 Treaty of St. Louis was significantly flawed, and the Band harbored legitimate arguments against its validity, which, if considered, might have undermined its enforcement. But like so many treaties with Native Americans in those days, arguments on their behalf fell on deaf ears, and the government determined it necessary to take military action against the Band. It called all frontier militias in the region to mobilize and report to a central command headed by General Henry Atkinson. People named Abraham Lincoln, Winfield Scott, Zachary Taylor, and Jefferson Davis saddled up,

1. James Lewis, "Black Hawk War," Britannica Online Encyclopedia, accessed December 30, 2023, https://www.britannica.com/event/Black-Hawk-War.

packed, and prepared for action in the territory. With their proximity to Illinois, the Covington Militia, including David Wallace, prepared to join the campaign. It created a lot of excitement and activity, and young Lew Wallace was all eyes and ears to the preparations.

By this time, David Wallace was elected Indiana's lieutenant governor and commissioned Colonel Wallace for this militia. As described by Lew, his father's horse was prepared by his groom and trimmed in grey cloth with a clean, polished saddle and tack. In addition, his father dressed in a blue frock coat with gold buttons and donned a half-moon hat adorned with plumes. Lew would describe many men as similarly dressed (although there was no standard uniform for the militia) with their horses smartly tacked. They carried muskets, swords, various other weaponry, and saddlebags packed with food, powder, and shot for an extended and aggressive campaign. As the men gathered, base drums in town beat a slow and determined cadence. Lew watched intently as a group of men clustered and moved toward his home. His father exited their front door, walked resolutely to his horse, mounted, and spurred his mount to lead the men in a departing parade through the town center. The procession moved at a protracted pace that lasted for some time. The drums continued to beat, and many onlookers waved and wept until the militia had slipped away from view and the drums ceased their tempo.

Young Lew thought it the most exhilarating performance he had ever witnessed, resolving that he would march to war if given the opportunity. He would do that on two occasions in his life, and after serving in two significant military campaigns that included negative and traumatic experiences, his resolution never wavered. At the beginning of the Spanish-American War in 1898, Lew petitioned the United States War Office to allow him to recruit a force and lead them against the Spanish at the age of seventy-one. The war office turned him down, and in a typical show of defiance in the face of rejection, Lew proceeded to a local recruiting office and insisted on enlisting as a private. The local recruiters refused him, presumably based on age. Lew then requested and was granted the opportunity to address local recruits before they departed Crawfordsville. Until his death, one could say Lew was the embodiment of the American fighting spirit. However, he often appeared more enamored with war's excitement, pomp, and circumstance than simply answering a call of duty.

The Schoolmaster Disappears

The US government and local militias quickly dispatched the Black Hawk War. After two major and some minor engagements, the Band was cornered in southern Wisconsin and surrendered. Chief Black Hawk was arrested and sentenced to a year in jail for his transgressions. The rest of the Band was forced to return to the Iowa Indian Territory, which was good news for the region. At the same time, there was better news for young Lew. The schoolmaster and his instruments of terror disappeared from the town's little red schoolhouse. All the boys were thrilled but soon taken aback when a woman arrived to replace him. How could they submit to a woman? Lew later acknowledged that his old schoolmaster taught him to read, but his new female teacher opened a larger world of wonder. Instead of rods, she laid two books in his hands, one of arithmetic and the other geography—the former rarely opened and the latter continuously. This new interest in geography and the accompanying maps would remain a constant throughout his education and later life. He would someday use his mapping and geographic skills to describe one of the world's most significant historical and religiously important regions in nearly exact and mesmerizing detail years before he ever visited it.

With Lew's newfound drawing skills, passion for military engagements, and fondness for geographical maps (not to mention increased opportunity due to truancy), the woods, streams, and fields surrounding Covington became his constant creative playground. Lew would observe that his time as a young child seemed to pass endlessly. For days, he and his friends became characters from history and literature and set about in make-believe travel, campaigns, chases, and battles. They reenacted the trips and escapades of historical figures like Columbus and Magellan with made-up costumes, vessels, and imaginary weapons. About this time, the servant girl whom Lew first met near the city's gallows joined the group for their magical campaign. She once again proved a frightful source of local information, including folklore, superstitions, ghosts, witch's brew, and other implausible yarn disturbing to her gullible young friends. As a result, Lew developed a fear of ghosts and other dreadful creatures alleged to be lurking in the nearby forests that limited his play to daytime hours.

Mother, Mother!

Although his ghostly fears were based on fiction, real tragedy would again befall Lew and the young Wallace family. Lew's mother, Esther, whom a family friend described as a woman who could sing and dance from Sunday to Sunday, died of "Galloping Consumption."[1] His father was in New York on business, and one of the women attending Esther called Lew to her bedside. His older brother was already present in tears. He wrote he was not fully aware of the moment, but he called for her, "Mother, mother!" but did not receive a familiar response. She was gone. The illness had come so quickly and aggressively that the boy hadn't time to prepare himself for the loss. Her death was bewildering and devastating—so blunt that Lew claimed many more deaths he witnessed never equaled the devastating effect.[2]

Their father was away, and their mother was gone. One can only imagine Lew's angst between her death and his father's return to Covington. He uses "Esther" as a main character in his most historical novel. In the storyline, she is the daughter of Simonides, a servant in the House of Hur, and a love interest of the main character, Judah Ben Hur. Interestingly, one could imagine a wealthy Israelite during the time of Christ referring to someone like Esther as a servant girl. Maybe Lew, upon later reflection, had more interest and respect for the Covington servant girl than he ever expressed.

---

1. Galloping Consumption is an especially virulent form of tuberculosis. The effects of the disease were progressive and almost always ended in death. Even today, now commonly known as acute tuberculosis, the condition is significantly resistant to drug therapy.

2. Wallace, *An Autobiography, Vol. 1*, 33.

After his mother's funeral, Lew and his brothers were taken to live in the home of Mr. and Mrs. John Hawkins, the parents of the future Mrs. Major General Edward S. Canby (Louisa) and Brigadier General John Parker Hawkins. Canby and Hawkins graduated from West Point and served with distinction during the Civil War. As brothers-in-law, Canby and Hawkins participated in the Battle of Fort Blakely, the war's last major battle between April 2 and April 9, 1865. Fort Blakely was located six miles north of Spanish Fort, Alabama, in Baldwin County and was a primary target of the Mobile Campaign. The surrender of the Fort on April 9 occurred shortly after Lee's surrender at Appomattox on the morning of the same day. Canby was commander of the Army of West Mississippi. Hawkins participated as commander of a brigade of the United States Colored Troops (USCT) and oversaw the District of Northeastern Louisiana. Subsequently, on April 12, Mobile would be occupied, and all significant hostilities ended.[3]

During the challenging time of his mother's passing in 1834, Lew could never have imagined he had entered the home of future generals. Lew's already substantial military and political connections expanded to assist in support of his future ambitions.

---

3. American Battlefield Trust, "Fort Blakley and Spanish Fort," accessed December 30, 2023, https://www.battlefields.org/learn/articles/fort-blakeley-and-spanish-fort.

Wabash College

It was 1836, two years had passed since the death of Lew's mother and his living at the Hawkins' house. Lew was now age nine but no less impetuous. So, it was an unwelcome surprise that his older brother William, age ten or eleven, was being sent to preparatory school at Wabash College in Crawfordsville. In those days, colleges like Wabash were different from today. They were much smaller and more focused in their areas of study, but they also served as preparatory schools for young boys later seeking advanced studies. Some preparatory students continued to higher levels at Wabash or moved to other advanced institutions. Many chose to enter seminary colleges.

Lew had a close relationship with his older brother, and soon after William's departure, it became an untenable strain on Lew's already battered sense of family security. Without planning or consideration, he decided to join his brother. Lew never thought he might need his father's permission, so he didn't ask.

Lew discovered his Uncle Milton—a few years older but not wiser— had planned a trip to Crawfordsville on horseback, and Lew strategized how to join him. On the morning of his young uncle's scheduled departure, Lew hiked through fields, woods, and thickets to hide about two to three miles out of Covington alongside the road to Crawfordsville. He figured he would ambush Uncle Milton and plead to go with him. After all, what would happen if Lew tried to walk back on his own and got lost? He sprang his trap upon the unsuspecting traveler, and after some begging, his uncle laughed and helped him aboard to ride double to Crawfordsville. Lew was on his way to college without knowing what that meant. He had no proper clothes, shoes, money, food, or anything of value. He did carry one valuable inanimate, which would often prove key to opening doors for him: his father's surname.

It was late afternoon before the double riders pulled up to the dugout basement door below a house, essentially the college. Their transportation had been an overweight, broad pony that was inordinately slow and added to her considerable riding discomfort. But she had covered the thirty miles in less than a day, and her riders were appreciative. After knocking on the door, Lew was greeted by an amiable man known as Uncle John Beard, the proprietor. Beard was followed by a woman, some children, and six boys, who appeared to be students. After several questions, he was recognized as Lieutenant Governor David Wallace's son and told that his brother William would be fetched.

Lew's appearance and unlikely request must have been comical, but he didn't appreciate the teasing he received from the students. Lew was allowed to stay but was soon transferred to an Episcopalian seminary outside Crawfordsville, more appropriate for his age. Again, he was treated to a daily diet of corporal punishment by the reverend running the school. Between the unwanted distractions that Lew knew as "class time," he could hear and then focused intently on the sound of flowing water.

My Friends

Soon after arriving at the seminary, Lew made two friends: a little river and a local farmer named Beeler. Lew described himself as ragged, unwashed, and probably pitied by the good-hearted Mr. Beeler, possibly a Whig who voted for his father.[1] Mr. Beeler had two possessions most attractive to Lew: an apple orchard and a canoe. As he had in Covington, Lew established a friendship with a man who would look after him and provide the opportunity to occupy himself along another engaging waterway. That little river is known today as Sugar Creek. It is one of Indiana's more popular canoeing and kayaking waterways, full of rising cliffs, rocks, and rapids, with sometimes dangerous undercurrents. It is beautiful and has provided thousands of people tranquil enjoyment over the years, and for many unfortunate others who failed to heed its danger, death by drowning.

Each day, Lew visited Beeler, and Beeler asked whether the reverend thrashed him. Lew usually answered in the affirmative and showed the welts on his legs. Beeler would flush red and suggest Lew invite the reverend down to his home so that he could give the man a taste of his own medicine. I'm sure the reverend knew not to venture in Beeler's direction whether Lew ever asked him. Instead, Beeler allowed Lew to use his canoe whenever asked, imposing only two demands on the nine-year-old:

---

1. Whig was originally short for Whiggamore, meaning "cattle driver," and used to describe western Scots who came to Leith, Scotland, for corn. The American Whig Party's main competitor was the Democratic Party, which was more dominant in the United States at the time.

"Don't drown and return the paddle." Lew always accomplished both and was invited to supper most evenings. It's interesting to note amid strict and dangerous environments, young Lew Wallace found kinship with kind older men and solace with rivers. One can only deduce he was an extraordinary youth, possessing personal skills far beyond his age, with little fear of engaging elders who protected, nurtured, and cared for him. Also, experiencing nature with its tranquility, power, and natural healing qualities brought him peace.

Lew's father soon became aware of Lew's attendance (or lack thereof) at the seminary and canoeing escapades along the creek. There was a family in Crawfordsville by the name of Kerr. They were acquaintances, and Lew's father discovered they had moved to a farm six miles north and needed assistance. David Wallace convinced them to foreman his wandering son for good use. Lew embraced the move to the country and quickly made friends with the youngest of the family, who sported a hunting rifle. Instead of burdening himself with the mundane chores of farming, Lew spent his days becoming an accurate marksman and successful hunter. After realizing his quickly developed skill and his deliverance of abundant fresh game to the dinner table, the Kerrs encouraged Lew in his new adventure by ignoring his lack of work and providing him with adequate ammunition. Although Lew found these times most enjoyable, he desired a return to town, the boarding-house with his brother, and the opportunity to read from its library. His father agreed he could return to Wabash.

Lew's return was short-lived, as one day, his brother summoned him to a local tavern to meet his father and new mother. David Wallace had taken a wife, Zerelda G. Sanders, the eldest daughter of a new and prominent physician in Indianapolis. They married at a low-key private hotel gathering in Indianapolis on December 26, 1836. His father and stepmother were moving to Crawfordsville, and he and his brothers were united again under one roof. Lew's father established a new law office and renewed his practice with fresh enthusiasm while at the same time campaigning for governor. Lew initially rejected his new mother, but eventually, the woman endeared herself, and Lew later referred to her as; "Mother Wallace, the sweet-tongued apostle of temperance and reform."

While remembering many women in his life like his mother Esther, Mrs. Hawkins, Mrs. Kerr, his stepmother Zerelda, and his wife Susan, Lew wrote near his final days, "I would like it clearly understood how profound my respect and reverence are for good women. The feeling is owing, perhaps, to my falling so often into the care of so many of them."[2]

---

2. Wallace, *An Autobiography, Vol 1*, 43.

The Panic of 1837

When Lew was almost ten, his father was elected governor of Indiana. The family moved to Indianapolis while the still-fledgling United States of America was falling into its first significant economic depression. The country had some downturns or recessions before, but nothing to the magnitude of 1837. Today, when people think of depressions, they think mainly of 1929 through 1941. But there have been others, and the depression of 1837 was so severe that it became known as the "Panic of 1837," lasting at least seven years. The domestic and international economic forces at work before and during this period would require a book of its own to explain, for which there are many to choose from should one be so inclined. Suffice it to say, it was significant and all-encompassing across all states, territories, and markets.[1]

From a political standpoint, the important result of the Panic of 1837 was that Democratic President Andrew Jackson and his successor, Democrat Martin Van Buren, received much criticism and blame for the banking and market failures that resulted and persisted. First, the Democrats accused the bankers, while the Whigs pointed the finger at the Democrats—specifically Jackson for refusing to renew the Bank of the United States charter in 1833. Then, they impugned Van Buren for refusing to use government intervention to address the crisis, such as emergency relief and increased spending on public infrastructure projects

---

1. The Economic Historian, "Panic of 1837," accessed December 30, 2023, https://economic-historian.com/2020/11/panic-of-1837/.

to reduce unemployment. These are the same, or very similar, political and economic controversies we've experienced in the United States and worldwide in modern times, such as the financial crisis of 2007-2009 and the COVID-19 pandemic of 2020-2022.

Due to the Panic of 1837, the price of rice and cotton tanked precipitously and took a long time to recover. The Southern economy was heavily dependent on these two commodities. The wealthy and powerful began questioning the efficacy of the United States government and its dominant ruling party. The overall effects benefited the new Indiana governor, David Wallace, as westward expansion accelerated, and the Whigs grew in political influence while the Democratic Party weakened. Unfortunately, Southern hostility and seeds of sedition grew. Before these could culminate into insurrection and succession, a war would be fought with Mexico from 1846 to 1848. The result garnered vast new territories for greater westward expansion, and a major gold rush in California in 1849 infused large deposits of new wealth into the country's banking system. Just as the still-young country began to settle in and profit from its newly acquired territories and wealth, run-on-banks culminated another major depression, the Panic of 1857.[2]

Unlike 1837, during and after 1857, the price of cotton remained relatively stable, and as a result, the Southern economy suffered comparatively less. Consequently, Southern aristocrats further questioned their need for what they perceived as an oppressive and incompetent federal government. The prevailing historical opinion is the Civil War was fought primarily to abolish slavery and this is true. Still, many at the time and today have not overlooked other issues, like the desire for individual state control and increased economic stability. Living through these tumultuous times must have influenced a young but highly astute Lew Wallace, but it is difficult to deduce. His autobiography never mentions them. However, wealth and the loss or gain, or regaining, plays a significant role in the story of *Ben Hur* and the life of Lew Wallace.

---

2. The Economic Historian, "Panic of 1857," accessed December 30, 2023, https://economic-historian.com/2020/07/panic-of-1857/ : The Panic of 1857 ended a period of prosperity and speculation following the Mexican-American War and the discovery of gold in California in the late 1840s. Gold pouring into the American economy played its part. The panic started with the failure of the New York City branch of the Ohio Life Insurance Co.

Hoosier Capital

David Wallace and his family resided in the newly acquired governor's home in Indianapolis in early 1837. Lew described the home as a convenient but plain dwelling. He further expressed his new life in Indianapolis in mundane terms:

> *My life in Indianapolis, it must be said, became more regular and tame, a result due in part to the authority sternly exercised by my father, but mostly to the gentler, if not wiser, the influence of my stepmother, who, by looking after me, keeping me washed, combed, and well clad, gradually initiated me into the comforts of a home intelligently managed. She was a member of the Christian Church and insisted upon my attendance once every Sunday. I fear the services failed to impress me as she desired.*[1]

Lew spent most of his time in church using his black oil-cloth church cap as a drawing tablet, utilizing a pencil, and sketching the faces of the congregation's most interesting characters. Not exactly how many people would imagine the future writer of a religiously influential novel spent his time with the Lord.

Shortly after the move to Indianapolis, a now ten-year-old Lew befriended another benevolent older man named Jacob Cox. Mr. Cox periodically set aside his tinner trade to pursue his lifelong dream of being

---

1. Wallace, *An Autobiography, Vol 1*, 48.

an artist, using primarily pigmented oil and canvas as mediums.[2] Mr. Cox returned to tinning when maintaining a decent living necessitated it. Upon hearing of his father sitting for a governor's portrait, Lew stumbled into Cox's studio, for which he was quickly forgiven and engaged to observe. Lew was confident Mr. Cox would have let him paint in the studio. However, due to his lack of experience and bravery to ask, he decided to abscond with some of Cox's paint. He positioned it on a clean tin plate, hurried home, plucked some hairs from a dog's tail to fashion a brush, stole some castor oil from a sick servant girl, found a blank wooden board to paint on, and chose Black Hawk the Indian chief from the Black Hawk War as his first subject. He utilized an image of him from a book in his father's collection.

His stepmother quickly recognized young Lew's sudden absence from regular home gatherings. When her survey of possible hiding places failed to locate him, it did uncover the chief's unfinished portrait. Mrs. Wallace decided to unveil it at a full family gathering, and Lew was horrified. He expected immediate wrath from his father but instead received a long and hearty laugh, followed by a man-to-man discussion. His father strongly suggested that pursuing an artisan trade in a city such as Indianapolis, which had few families of wealth at the time, would result in little more than a life of poverty. Lew's feeble attempt to argue that Mr. Cox practiced such a trade was quickly discarded with the reminder that he had another trade, which provided his living. Lew was advised to put his time and emphasis back into schoolwork and forget about art, which he naturally ignored. He continued sketching and painting, practicing these favorite past times while continuing to perform the art of truancy—which he had nearly perfected.

Lew soon developed another passion: libraries and reading. Shortly after arriving in the capital, he became the most often listed visitor at the state library—which later served him in his writing career. Lew mentioned two books that attracted his attention at a time he described as the most impressionable period of his life. They were *Astoria* and *The Last of the Mohicans*, the first by Washington Irving and the latter by James

---

2. A tinner, also referred to as a tinsmith, is a person who makes and repairs things made of tin or other light metals. The same word may also refer to an unrelated specialty of iron-smithing.

Fennimore Cooper.[3] *Astoria* is most interesting when considering Lew's writing style in *Ben Hur*. Irving describes the new Oregon Territory in extraordinary detail. He describes it with such romanticism and grandeur that thousands of people over the next few decades uproot and attempt the long and treacherous journey over the Oregon Trail to settle.[4] An estimated 20,000 souls died in the attempt, and thousands of others quit along the way. Some years later, Irving revealed he never visited Oregon, even after the publishing of *Astoria*.

---

3. Wallace, *An Autobiography, Vol 1*, 54 : Washington Irving completed the *Astoria* manuscript in two months in the late summer of 1835, relying on the work of Thomas McKenney, the US Superintendent of Indian Trade during the 1820s, the journals of Meriwether Lewis and William Clark, explorer Steven Long, and traders Ross Cox and Gabriel Franchére, 1766.

4. The Oregon Trail began at Independence, Missouri, and traversed west by northwest over 2,170 miles to the mouth of the Columbia River on the Pacific Coast.

Centerville

Lew was a significant discipline challenge to his father and stepmother for the next few years. Eventually, his father relocated him and his elder brother to his aunt's home in Centerville, Indiana. Lew's father had heard of a teacher there of high repute who would change his son's educational perspective forever. Lew wrote about his new teacher with admiration and appreciation:

> *Professor Samuel K. Hoshour—his name purposely given in full—came more nearly to my ideal schoolmaster than any to whose tender mercies it had been my lot to fall. He wielded the rod and vigorously, but with discrimination and undeniable justice, and really taught me. He even interested me in arithmetic. Getting me to his house of evenings, with infinite patience, he would cipher me over the knottier problems, explaining the rules pencil in hand. Better evidence of Christian nature no man can furnish.*[1]

Professor Hoshour was likely the first to have recognized Lew's writing potential. He impressed upon him examples of what he considered the essence of the art; "In writing, everything is to be sacrificed to clearness of expression-everything."[2] Hoshour introduced the lectures of John Quincy Adams, writings by Irish authors Sir Richard Steele and Oliver

1. Wallace, *An Autobiography, Vol. 1*, 56.
2. Ibid., 57.

Goldsmith, Shakespeare, old Isaiah, and most importantly, the New Testament. "There," Hoshour said to Lew, "read that. It is the story of the birth of Jesus Christ".[3] Lew found the story fascinating while at the same time noting the relatively brief discussion of the wise men. Later, he filled this perceived gap with his own narrative and paid special homage to his beloved professor in his autobiography.[4] "The year (in Centerville) was the turning point of my life, and out of my age and across his grave I send him, Gentle master, hail and all sweet rest! Now I know wherein I am most obliged to you-unconsciously, perhaps, but certainly, you taught me how to educate myself up to every practical need."[5]

Lew may have met Oliver P. Morton while in Centerville in 1840. Although four years older than Lew, Morton attended Hoshour's academy for a time but worked in town as a hatter's apprentice while Lew was there.[6] Morton became governor of Indiana during the Civil War.[7] He was a strong promoter of Lew's military aspirations when the war began. However, not long after the Battle of Shiloh, Morton bent to political pressure and turned against him, removing Lew from his field command. As a result, many believe Governor Morton became a marginally veiled friend turned traitorous character in *Ben Hur*.

After only a year with Professor Hoshour, Lew returned home to Indianapolis to reenter his previous seminary. This time, however, he was a more serious student. He joined a literary society and began writing stories to be shared with his fellow members, and his first work he titled *The Man-at-Arms: A Tale of the Tenth Century*. It was the first time Lew showed an interest in Spain and depicted Spaniards as gallant knights and warriors. The main character was named "Pedro"; his love interest was known as the "Rose of Guadalajara." Although admittedly rudimentary and amateurish, the story was similar to what Lew would eventually produce for a professional publication, full of detailed descriptions of a foreign romantic land with heaps of dynamic bravado.

---

3. Ibid., 58.

4. In *Ben Hur*, Wallace dramatically expands the story of the wise men compared to the Bible's version. He integrates them into the story after the birth of Christ and gives them identities with unique personalities. It is a detailed, fascinating creation with lasting effect by Lew Wallace.

5. Wallace, *An Autobiography, Vol.1*, 59.

6. A hatter is someone who makes and sells hats.

7. Indiana Historical Bureau, "Indiana Governor Oliver Perry Morton," accessed January 11, 2024, https://www.in.gov /history/about-indiana-history-and-trivia/governors-portraits/list-of-governors/indiana-governor-oliver-perry-morton-1823 –1877/.

First Attempt

Sometime in 1843, when Lew was sixteen years old, he read about the Texas War of Independence against Mexico. Legends like Crockett, Travis, Houston, and Bowie were spreading, and Lew was anxious to run off and join the fight. He subsequently secured firearms, a sizeable bowie-shaped knife, and a skiff with a friend. They planned to launch on the White River and traverse the river system to New Orleans to meet Commodore Moore, who they were sure would make them midshipmen. To their surprise, nearly the entire seminary student body learned of their plans and showed up at the river to see them off. They launched to supportive cheers, but news of their plan quickly made its way to Lew's father, and Lew was apprehended by a constable about ten miles south of the city while happily gathering firewood. This was Lew's first of five attempts to join a war, three involving Mexico and three ultimately unsuccessful.

A few days passed, and Lew's father called him into the library for a serious discussion. Lew met something in his father's library that Lew's adversaries also met during Lew's lifetime: serious, intense, penetrating, black eyes. Like many said in later years about Lew, "Once you've seen them, you don't forget them."[1] Lew's reaction to his father's dark glare would be no exception as his father said:

> *I have struggled to give you and your brothers what, in my opin-*
> *ion, is better than money—education. Since your sixth year, I*

---

1. Alexander "Homer" Bonnell to Michael E. Fox at the Green Street Barber Shop in Crawfordsville, IN, circa 1966.

have paid school bills for you, but one day you will regret the opportunities you have willfully thrown away. I am sorry, disappointed, mortified; so, without shutting the door upon you, I am resolved that from today you must go out and earn your own livelihood. I shall watch your course hopefully. That is all I have to say.[2]

One might think that Lew viewed this as a sad ending to his childhood, but they would be wrong. If you believe Lew, he was elated, welcoming that his father had finally given him his freedom.

2. Wallace, *An Autobiography,* Vol.1, 78.

County Clerk

Out of the gate into the street, never to return except as a guest! I very much fear there was lacking in me the proper appreciation of the solemnity and uncertainties of the crisis.

—LEW WALLACE[1]

A sixteen-year-old Lew was given his freedom and sent out into the world by his father to make a living and future for himself. He had a self-professed spring in his step as he left the family home. However, it didn't take long as he walked towards downtown to realize he needed a source of income—and the sooner, the better. His first stop was the county clerk's office. He already knew someone there, the county clerk, Robert S. Duncan. When Lew asked Mr. Duncan for a job, Mr. Duncan gave him a quizzical look, "You want to settle down, do you?"

Undeterred by the insinuation, Lew answered, "Yes, if I can."

"You can. Come with me," Mr. Duncan replied.[2]

So, with that notably brief job interview, Lew started his career as a clerk and learned to make complete legal records.

It's important to note that the first place Lew stopped after leaving his home was related to the legal profession—a profession practiced by his maternal grandfather and father. As unconventional as Lew might have

---

1. Ibid., 84.
2. Ibid., 85.

seemed at the time, his choice of employment was very traditional, given his family's history. In addition, upon venturing out on his own, Lew was again befriended, fed, and protected by another kind older gentleman. Lew remarked that Mr. Duncan had "patience with him impossible to forget."[3] He stood at a table and initiated Lew into the mysteries of captions, pleadings, orders, judgments, and dates of filing, saying at the end of the lesson, "Now, I'll give you ten cents for every hundred words you write, so that how much you'll make will depend on yourself."[4] He soon made enough money to pay rent at a boarding house and buy food, clothing, and a rifle to kill fresh game. He and Mr. Duncan often hunted together, and Lew became a very comfortable, traditional young man. It's curious to observe Lew be one thing (rebellious and untraditional), at which point, upon getting what he wants, he quickly adapts to the contrary.

3. Ibid., 85.
4. Ibid., 85.

Self-Education

After a few months, Lew became proficient at writing and creating official county files. He could easily write 3,000 words in a regular workday, guaranteeing him at least fifteen dollars per week in income. But as time passed, Lew became bored with just the writing work. Having never forgotten Professor Hoshour's influence in Centerville, he set about educating himself and began experimenting with writing styles and topics. He continued to visit the state and his father's library, which his father kept well stocked with the latest periodicals from around the world and the newest book publications. One day, Lew came upon a new book by William H. Prescott, just delivered to his father, *History of the Conquest of Mexico*[1]. Born in Massachusetts and educated at Harvard, Prescott is considered the world's first "scientific historian" and is also known as a "Hispanist historian." His works were about the Hispanic regions of North and South America. In addition to being a gifted researcher, writer, and scholar, Prescott was a dramatic storyteller.[2]

The History of the Conquest of Mexico is still considered an epic piece of historical literature. It had everything Lew always dreamed of and reenacted in the forests surrounding Covington. A book about the Spanish conquistador Hernán Cortés, who, in the act of open mutiny, sailed from Cuba in 1519 with a small army of men, landed on the Yucatan

1. Ibid., 88–89.
2. Wilbur R. Jacobs, "William H. Prescot, American historian," Britanica Online Encyclopedia, accessed January 12, 2024, https://www.britannica.com/biography/William-H-Prescott.

Peninsula, quickly conquered the Maya civilization, then moved south to Veracruz. From there, Cortés proceeded west to what is now Mexico City, where, together with approximately 1,000 indigenous people, he recruited and converted to Catholicism along the way, completely dismantling the Aztec empire. Consequently, acting under a self-created authority, Cortés brought most of modern-day Mexico under the rule of the king of Castile in Spain. Lew described Prescott's book as adventure, combat, heroism, and religion in mortal issue. Similar words are often used to describe *Ben Hur*.

Some historians have made the error of concluding that Lew Wallace's book *The Fair God, or The Last of the 'Tzins: A Tale of the Conquest of Mexico,* was written and published after *Ben Hur*. This is not the case. *The Fair God* was initially started long before, sometime around 1843, when Lew was only sixteen. It was picked up, worked on, and reworked many times and eventually published in 1873, seven years before his greatest novel. The first publishing brought moderate sales. After the tremendous success of *Ben Hur*, Lew Wallace came to fame, and *The Fair God* was republished and experienced more significant sales. He wrote and published other books after that. Regardless of the specific details or timing, it was most certainly William H. Prescott who first spellbound Lew Wallace with historical drama and inspired him to start writing in earnest. It was not the birth of Christ or the Holy Land that first mesmerized him, but rather Mexico and the pagan, highly advanced civilizations.

PART 2

The Mexican-American War

[T]he officers of the army were indifferent whether the annexation was consummated or not, but not so all of them. For myself, I was bitterly opposed to the measure, and to this day, regard the War, which resulted, as one of the most unjust ever waged by a stronger nation against a weaker nation. It was an instance of a republic following the bad example of European monarchies, in not considering justice in their desire to acquire additional territories.

—President Ulysses S. Grant[1]

---

1. Ulysses S. Grant, *Personal Memoirs of General U. S. Grant Vol. 1,* (Charles L. Webster & Company, 1885), 16.

Marion Rifles

At seventeen, Lew had his first opportunity to taste military culture. A West Point graduate started a new volunteer company called the City Greys in Indianapolis. It was a local militia initially intended by the United States Constitution's Second Amendment, so they were regulated by military rules and regulations, wore standard uniforms, and carried military muskets with bayonets. The Greys comprised older men, some even tending towards middle age. Younger men like Lew wanted to join the militia, but the Greys were not obliging, so a second junior militia was formed, and they took the name of the Marion Rifles. Lew explained the Rifles were made up of young men mostly incapable of mustaches. In those days, having a mustache and beard was a moniker of manhood, so the Greys brutally teased and belittled the Rifles.

Planned or not, the Rifles exacted revenge on the Greys during a capital celebration downtown when a mock display of military confrontation was planned and performed. The Greys and Rifles were to shoot volleys of paper-wads at one another as they marched toward the simulated battle. The Rifles should've retreated after firing their volley, but their captain failed to give the order for some reason. After discharging their breech-loaders, the Rifles rose from their firing positions and charged the Greys.[1] One of the Greys was shot with a paper-wad at close

---

1. While the Greys used mainly muzzle-loading muskets that were the standard issue then and up to the Civil War, the Rifles most likely used the older M1819 Hall rifle, a single-shot breech-loading rifle adopted by the US Army dating back to 1819.

range, and the Rifles took several prisoners. The Greys were unhappy, but Lew and the others were ecstatic. If Lew had not been completely enamored with the idea of military battle before this experience, he now had an overwhelming passion. Having been elected a second sergeant, he took the position seriously. Sometime after the mock skirmish, Lew got a copy of General Winfield Scott's newly published *Infantry Tactics Vol. 1*. He described it as "Finding a diamond in the mud," putting everything aside to devour the manual.[2] Lew was determined to make himself a well-schooled military drillmaster, and he did within a short period.

---

2. Wallace, *An Autobiography Vol. 1*, 94.

Pretext for War

Before delving into Lew Wallace's involvement in the Mexican-American War, the reader should be provided background and perspective leading up to and including the conflict to understand better Lew's motivation for venturing to Mexico and lifetime defense of his participation. Today, most historians agree there was no clear, undisputed hostility, attack, or atrocity to justify a declaration of war. Over many years, incidents and conflicts, like the Alamo (1836), influenced opinions about Mexico and created legends for young men like Lew Wallace to emulate. Suffice it to say there was enough blame on both sides. But many of the legends and particulars were embellished by biased American journalists hoping to sell newspapers, pamphlets, and books. The Alamo occurred ten years before the Mexican-American War. It played out clearly within claimed Mexican territory, fought mainly by Texans, to create an independent country from Mexico. The Alamo had little to do with any Mexican-United States territory disputes at the time.

In 1836, most Texans wanted a separate independent country, not to become part of the United States. However, as more Americans migrated to Texas over the years, opinions started to change. By early 1845, it was generally thought public opinion in Texas favored annexation to the United States. But in 1845, Texas President Anson Jones, ambivalent to public opinion or annexation, sent a letter to Mexican President José Joaquín Herrera dated March 29. He proposed to Herrera that in return for Texas's independence from Mexico, Texas would entertain the idea she "not annex herself or become subject to any country whatsoever."[1]

On May 30, President Jones received a letter from President Herrera that contained a confirmed offer to recognize Texas as separate from Mexico, provided Texas never joined another country. Nevertheless, by the time Herrera's letter arrived, public pressure had accelerated in Texas, instigated and agitated by the United States to accept an offer of annexation passed by Congress and signed by President James K. Polk two months earlier in March of 1845. Jones now had a dilemma and did not act on Herrera's offer. Instead, in late June, the Texas Congress acted for him by accepting the annexation, which included full statehood. The vote was unanimous.

It's important to inject into the narrative the history before President Polk took office. In 1840, the longtime Wallace family friend and fellow Whig, William Henry Harrison, ran for president and defeated incumbent Martin Van Buren. His ticket was a "quasi split-ticket" as his running mate John Tyler, initially a Democrat, later opposed Democratic Jacksonian Policies and became estranged from the party. Tyler tended to throw his support behind the Whigs, and they saw him as an opportunity to gain Southern support since Tyler was from a slave-owning Virginia family and Harrison was viewed as anti-slavery. Harrison and Tyler ran on the now-famous slogan, "Tippecanoe and Tyler Too." Thirty-one days into his presidency, Harrison succumbed to pneumonia, and Tyler became the first president to succeed to the presidency.

Tyler's succession was questioned by his cabinet, which initially wanted to swear him in as vice president-acting president, but Tyler pushed back and eventually won out.[2] His leadership was unremarkable and little remembered, leading to the Democrats reestablishing power in 1845. However, Tyler was always on the same page as the Democrats regarding annexing Texas. In fact, as a lame-duck president, he signed a bill to offer Texas statehood, which the Democrats later transformed into annexation. Harrison's untimely passing creates an interesting question: if Harrison

1. Justin H. Smith, *The Annexation of Texas*, Barnes & Noble, 2022 (Orig. Publ. University of Virginia 1941), 410.

2. The White House, "John Tyler, The 10th President of the United States," accessed January 12, 2024, https://www.whitehouse.gov/about-the-white-house/presidents/john-tyler/.

had survived his presidency, would he have moved Congress and the country away from a war with Mexico, thereby altering Lew's opinion of the war, not to mention the history and borders of the United States?

By early 1846, before a declaration of war and the beginning of hostilities, many United States Army officers were indifferent toward war to settle a Texas border dispute with Mexico. Most of the Whigs in Congress were against it, but President Polk and House Democrats had a different view. First, it was extremely tempting and made economic and strategic sense to annex Texas and acquire New Mexico and California, which they originally wanted. Second, the United States needed territory to expand and ports on the pacific coast. Third, there was a common belief that Mexico was too poor and the central government was too remote to protect and develop these rich-resource territories adequately. The United States had more wealth and an abundance of people flowing into its borders to settle and fill the regions, properly utilize them, and make them more productive. It also had a military capable of taming hostile lands and securing them for continued development.

In addition, it was believed by many in Washington that if Texas took President Herrera up on his offer and became an independent country, it would create a security threat to the United States. The country was currently embroiled in a territorial dispute with England over the Oregon Territory, and England was beating their war drums. Suppose England decided to start a war against the United States in the Northwest and, at the same time, invade or blockade a newly formed independent Texas. In that case, the United States could be battling England on two fronts: a long way from Washington and existing supply lines. In addition, England would have support from Canada to the north and, most likely, Mexico to the south. The United States knew it could easily defeat Mexico to achieve its territorial goals, but it was different to battle England on two fronts. In the eyes of President Polk, acquiring Texas, New Mexico, and California was critical to counter the possible threats. His overall objectives were reasonable and well-grounded, but many felt a bloody war with Mexico was unnecessary to realize those objectives.

It goes undisputed the war was controversial and bitterly debated in the United States. Although the Democratically-controlled Congress voted in favor of it in May of 1846, the Senate and House Whigs challenged the honesty of Polk's claims that Mexico had invaded US-claimed territory. In return, Polk accused the Whigs of treason. Polk claimed that Mexico, in April of 1846, had "invaded our territory and shed American blood on American soil" in a military attack on United States troops in Texas under the command of Zachary Taylor, killing or injuring sixteen soldiers in an area between the Nueces and the Rio Grande Rivers.[3] Everyone knew this was a highly flammable and disputed border area—a dispute created by the annexation of Texas. From the Mexican perspective, the first incident of aggression was the illegal foreign theft of Mexican territory. Mexico refused to acknowledge the annexation, expelled all United States diplomats from Mexico, and ceased formal relations.

After the declaration of war was passed and hostilities had commenced, Whig congressmen and senators continued challenging Polk and Taylor's details of the Mexican incident. It became known that Polk sent John Slidell to Mexico City in September 1845 on a secret mission to negotiate the disputed border, settle US claims against Mexico, and purchase Texas, New Mexico, and California for up to $30 million. When Slidell arrived, the president of Mexico refused to receive him, and Polk was incensed by the Mexican snub. In January 1847, the Whigs took control of the House and voted 85 to 81 to censure Polk for "unnecessarily and unconstitutionally initiating a war with Mexico."[4] People like Abraham Lincoln, who at the time was a Whig party congressman from Illinois, bitterly debated the declaration in the House and introduced eight "spot" resolutions, which placed the truthfulness of Polk's claim under scrutiny and preserved for historical purposes Polk's lack of specific details.[5] Lincoln immediately became and remained a national hero in Mexico for his efforts to stop the war. However, the House did not act on Lincoln's resolutions, and Polk and Taylor remained steadfast in their claims. As a result, the war proceeded, and by 1847, it was impossible to reverse.

---

3. Adam Zeidan, "Invasion and War," Britannica Online Encyclopedia, accessed September 2, 2023, https://www.britannica.com/event/Mexican-American-War/Invasion-and-war.

4. Ibid.

5. The resolutions requested President James K. Polk to provide Congress with the exact location (Spot) upon which blood was spilled on American soil, as Polk had claimed in 1846 when asking Congress to declare war on Mexico. Unfortunately, neither Polk nor Taylor provided information explicitly identifying the spot.

The famous author Henry David Thoreau became one of the most vocal war critics outside Washington. A passionate abolitionist, Thoreau opined the war was an attempt by the slave states to extend slavery and enhance their power by creating additional slave states out of the soon-to-be-stolen Mexican land. Thoreau was not alone in this assertion. Many abolitionists joined and supported his criticism of Southern Democrats, who strongly supported hostilities to acquire Mexican territory. Thoreau labeled the war as "immoral" and refused to pay six years of poll taxes in protest. As a result, the government put him in jail, but he only spent one night incarcerated, as his aunt paid his taxes against his wishes. Thoreau channeled his opposition and frustration with the war into a now famous and lengthy essay he wrote in 1894 titled *Civil Disobedience.* In the essay, Thoreau writes about injustices that governments sometimes engage where they are, "of such a nature that it requires you to be the agent of injustice to another, then, I say, break the law. Let your life be a counter friction to stop the machine."[6]

---

6. Henry David Thoreau, *Civil Disobedience : Complete Texts with Introduction, Historical Contexts, Critical Essays* (Houghton Mifflin, 2000), 25.

Studying Law

In his eighteenth year, what later became *The Fair God* grew in size and sophistication, as did Lew's maturation into manhood. He began to ask himself essential questions about the future. Being a clerk and a copyist was fine from sixteen to eighteen, but would this always be his vocation? For an enlightened young man like Lew Wallace, the answer was no. His older brother had started studying law in his father's office, and although Lew saw this as a natural step, he viewed a law office as a house of routine. As the son of a lawyer and working as a clerk and legal copyist, he knew the mundane writing and rewriting horrors of law practice. Lew never viewed it as a particularly interesting or noble profession. However, he was ambitious and knew law practice was a steppingstone to higher aspirations.

Without a view of the law as his ultimate career, Lew nonetheless made the pragmatic decision to join his brother in his father's law office, with the eventual goal of becoming a lawyer. Studying law in those days was a non-paying position. Although he did make some money working as a "pettifogger," much to his disgust, he would many times call on the kindness of his old friend Mr. Duncan in the clerk's office to provide work and income when needed.[1]

As Lew continued his law studies, events in Texas and Washington began to unfold, and he followed the published stories with great interest.

---

1. A pettifogger is an inferior legal practitioner, especially one who deals with petty cases or employs dubious practices. Although in 1846 Indiana, practicing as a pettifogger was not "per se" illegal, it was certainly looked down on by licensed attorneys and judges. Nonetheless, it was tolerated so young men studying law like Lew Wallace could earn money to support themselves once they had reached some level of "petti level competence."

As a result, he became convinced the looming Mexican-American War was justified. He was preparing to take the bar exam to garner his law license and applied through the Indiana Supreme Court. However, his study discipline was lacking. His mind wandered elsewhere whenever he tried to focus on the law books, and he mainly spent his time on *Scott's Infantry Tactics* and, occasionally, *The Fair God.* The exam was quickly approaching, and Lew was woefully unprepared. He was familiar with the examining judge, Isaac Blackford, and Blackford of him. There was perhaps some false hope that Justice Blackford's familiarity with his family name might garner him some favor despite his poor preparation.

Rather than reserve his right to a withdrawal, he decided to move forward and take the exam. Lew finished the exam before many of the others and took some of the extra time to write a small note to Justice Blackford, which was flippant at best and sealed his immediate future:

> *Hon. Isaac Blackford, Examining Judge: Dear Sir: I hope the forgoing answers will be to your satisfaction more than they are to mine.; whether they are or not, I shall go to Mexico.*
>
> *Respectfully, Lew Wallace.*[2]

Two or three days afterward, he received a response via mail in the form of a small note:

> *Mr. Lew Wallace;*
> *Dear Sir,*
> *The Court interposes no objection to your going to Mexico.*
>
> *Respectfully, Isaac Blackford.*[3]

There was no law license enclosed, and no further information was provided. So, with Blackford's response, Lew received official notice of his exam failure and, as a result, was left with three options: go to war, study law, or go back to being a county clerk.

The decision had already been made.

---

2. Wallace, *An Autobiography Vol. 1*, 112.
3. Ibid., 113.

Volunteering

On May 22, 1846, Governor Whitcomb called for military volunteers in Indiana, according to the Declaration of War with Mexico. However, Indiana was new to the concept of war, as it had only just become a state in 1816. There were few rules or processes in place to recruit volunteers. Lew, recognizing an opportunity and seeing no impediments, set up a recruiting station and enlisted an entire company of men within three days.[1] The company voted and elected a captain, first lieutenant, and second lieutenant. Lew was voted second lieutenant.[2] He was only nineteen but was the recruiter, organizer, and apparently qualified. In addition, Lew's initiative won him an officer's position. Shortly after, the governor accepted the company into the Indiana volunteers, and they received orders to proceed to the general rendezvous point located on the Ohio River on the Indiana side. Their initial transport would be wagons to a railhead in Edinburg, and then a train would take them to Madison. From Madison, they would march to Clarksville.

Lew remained stoic throughout the recruiting and volunteering process, but suddenly, his father appeared and marched alongside him toward the wagons. Lew recalled this about his father showing up that day: "Up to that he had kept silent, which was well enough, seeing I had only to look into his face to know he was proud of me and approved my going, then took my hand and said, 'Goodbye, come back a man.' Suddenly, I gave him a shower of tears."[3]

---

1. A company is a military unit, typically 80–250 soldiers, usually commanded by a major or a captain. Although the exact number may vary by unit type and structure, most companies have three to six platoons.

2. General Lew Wallace Study & Museum, "Lew Wallace in Mexico," accessed January 12, 2024, https://www.ben-hur.com/lew-wallace-in-mexico/.

3. Wallace, *An Autobiography Vol. 1*, 115.

Camp Clark

Falls of the Ohio State Park is an island in southern Indiana, located just below the northern banks of the Ohio River at Clarksville, Indiana, directly above Louisville, Kentucky. The park is also part of the Falls of the Ohio National Wildlife Conservation Area, and its main attraction is the exposed fossil beds dating back to the Devonian period.[1] At the falls and on this island, Lewis & Clark first rendezvoused to begin their now-famous expedition. It is also where three Indiana regiments assembled, organized, equipped, and mustered into national service to fight the Mexican-American War: the First, Second, and Third Indiana Infantry Regiments. Second Lieutenant Lewis Wallace and his Company H became part of the First Indiana Infantry Regiment.[2]

The regiment set about electing its officers. James P. Drake was elected colonel, Christian C. Nave lieutenant colonel, and Henry S. Lane from Crawfordsville as major. As a successful lawyer, Henry S. Lane eventually became governor of Indiana, a United States senator, president of the first Republican National Convention, and one of Abraham Lincoln's closest friends and allies. More importantly for Lew Wallace, Major Lane later became his brother-in-law. After the elections, the regiments came together and appropriately named the encampment "Camp Clark."

On July 5, 1846, the three Indiana regiments boarded river steamers at New Albany to transport them to New Orleans via the Ohio and the

---

1. In geologic time, the Devonian Period was between 419.2 million and 358.9 million years ago. Late in the period, the first four-legged amphibians appeared, indicating the colonization of land by vertebrates.

2. A regiment is a unit of an army typically commanded by a colonel and divided into several companies, squadrons, or batteries and often into two battalions. The three Mexican-American War Indiana regiments comprised 4 to 6 companies of about 160 men per company or 800 troops per regiment.

Mississippi. There, they would be assigned to a Baltimore clipper-built brig in New Orleans and sail to Brazos de Santiago, on the other side of the gulf, near the mouth of the Rio Grande River.[3] The first day and night of sailing were very uncomfortable. The weather conditions on the gulf turned rough, and the poor lads from Indiana—unaccustomed to ship travel—experienced severe seasickness. However, when the second day turned calm and progressed to a beautiful moonlit night, Lew experienced one of the most beautiful things: a brief yet memorable passing encounter with a ship. It was a three-mast merchantman, fully rigged, with every sail set.[4] Lew described it as "glacial white, mountain high, deathly still, a spectral, gliding glory of moonlight space [. . .]. When now and then the curious ask me of the beautiful things I have seen, even the most beautiful, I astonish them by honoring that ship."[5]

---

3. A clipper was a type of mid-nineteenth-century merchant sailing vessel designed for speed. Clippers were generally narrow for their length, small by later nineteenth-century standards, could carry limited bulk freight, and had a large total sail area. A brig is a sailing vessel with two square-rigged masts. During the Age of Sail, brigs were seen as fast and maneuverable and used as naval warships and merchant transports.

4. A vessel of three or more masts, fore, and aft, rigged on the aftermost mast and square-rigged on all others, is called a barque, sometimes spelled "bark." A merchantman refers to it as a commercial vessel instead of a military warship.

5. Wallace, *An Autobiography, Vol. 1*, 120.

Bagdad

Had we known in advance—I speak illustratively—what all of misery and humiliation there was awaiting us in that camp to which we now marched, I think it not unlikely that despair would have unloosed every bond of discipline and sunk our eight hundred good men into an ungovernable mob.

—LEW WALLACE[1]

The next morning, after Lew marveled at the passing ship, he was topside of the anchored brig, viewing the small inlet where Padre Island terminated, and the tip was known as Brazos de Santiago. He could only see a small hut with wooden barrels fashioned as a chimney and a small structure half-buried in sand and driftwood. There was no town, no grass, and no trees. It was an eye-opening sight for a young man from Indiana, where everywhere was thick with vegetation. However, tragedy didn't take long to touch Lew and First Indiana.

Upon landing, Lew's regiment was ordered to march ten miles north of the mouth of the Rio Grande. Shortly before reaching their destination and while on a rest break, Lew and two fellow soldiers, John Anderson and Luther Reck, ventured to the banks of the Rio Grande to seek relief from the oppressive weather. Anderson dared Lew and Reck to follow him into the river. The river was swollen from recent rains, and Lew

---

1. Ibid., 123.

described it as "angry looking." Lew reasoned to Anderson that it wasn't the tranquil White River of Indiana, and they should not risk it, but Anderson egged them on, and as venturesome young lads do, they swam towards the opposite bank. Soon, Reck began laboring and lagging. He suddenly screamed—possibly cramping—then sank like a stone, only to surface briefly before disappearing. Poor Reck was never recovered, probably quickly dispatched to the Gulf of Mexico. A report was filed, and a letter was sent to Reck's parents. Lew recalled it was weeks before he and Anderson could talk about the incident, and he reasoned Anderson felt more remorse as the instigator.[2] However, Lew writing the story of Judah Ben Hur saving Quintus Arrius from drowning after Macedonian pirates sank Arrius' magnificent battleship might have emerged from Lew's conscience-stricken memory of Reck.

Shortly after this tragedy, General Zachary Taylor ordered the regiment to return and garrison at the mouth of the Rio Grande, approximately eight miles south down the beach from the Brazos.[3] There was a makeshift camp, which they would inherit from the First Mississippi Volunteers, commanded by the future president of the Southern Confederacy, Jefferson Davis. The First Mississippi was boarding a steamer heading upriver as First Indiana arrived. Davis was anxious to move his troops towards Monterrey and the impending battle, where they fought with distinction. Lew's first reaction to the camp was a sense of utter desolation; to the north were numerous dunes a few hundred yards from the river, and to the south was flat emptiness that seemed to extend infinitum. This arid and treeless expanse offered no resistance to ocean tides or river overflow. Across the river was a small Mexican village previous soldiers had nicknamed "Bagdad" (historically misspelled), a reference to the Arabian story of *Ali Baba and the Forty Thieves of Baghdad.*[4] The small town harbored a group of Mexican smugglers, and therefore the reference connection.[5]

---

2. Ibid., 122.

3. Garrison is a term for any number of troops stationed in a particular location to guard it. The term applies to certain facilities that constitute a military base or fortified military headquarters.

4. *Ali Baba and the Forty Thieves of Baghdad* is a folk tale from *One Thousand and One Nights.* It was added to the collection in the eighteenth century by its French translator, Antoine Galland, who heard it from Syrian storyteller Hanna Diyab. Note: The Americans or Mexicans misspelled "Bagdad," which continues today.

5. The town embraced the name Bagdad and grew to a population of over 15,000 by the 1860's. Used as a haven by Confederates during and after the Civil War, it collapsed and was non-existent by 1880.

First Indiana began its dreadful experience with the military encampment. Their only water source came from the Rio Grande, consisting of about one-third sand and one-third yellow mud. The bacterial and salt content of the remaining one-third, drawn at the end of the waterway versus a source, can only be imagined. Their rations were dry beans, coffee, sugar, often rancid pickled pork, flour, and biscuits. The biscuits were replete with a type of brown bug. They could catch shrimp from the river, but any vegetable, even an onion, was unavailable.

It didn't take long before dysentery spread through the encampment. The regiment had one surgeon, so the soldiers nursed one another. Their medical supplies consisted mainly of bandages and opium tablets. Opium smooths muscle tone and decreases fluid secretion in the intestines, and when a soldier's condition deteriorated to near emaciated uselessness, he was dispensed the tablets and, most often, died shortly after. Soon, the corpses could not be buried in coffins, as the wood needed to make them was quickly exhausted. The wind blowing on the camp was intense and relentless, so after burying a corpse without a coffin, the body reappeared many times, fully exposed. The number of fallen kept the men busy all day with burial details and military honors. It served as a morbid distraction from dwelling on their miserable existence.

Lew admitted his touch with reality became attenuated, blocking reality with daydreams of long marches through beautiful valleys, occasional military engagements, and eventually arriving as conquerors in Mexico City. At the time, Mexico City was said to be the most beautiful capital in the world, and such daydreaming probably saved many a soldier's sanity.

Relief

In all my reading of American wars, the colonial included, I cannot recall another instance of a command so wantonly neglected and so brutally dislocated.

—LEW WALLACE[1]

After weeks of misery and so many deaths that Lew lost count, First Indiana received orders to proceed to General Taylor's headquarters in Walnut Springs near Monterey, Mexico. The sick would be left at a field hospital in Matamoros. The trip would require a riverboat ride of 210 miles to Ciudad Camargo and then a land march of 180 miles to Walnut Springs. The regiment couldn't pack fast enough for movement. There was tremendous relief, and they soon began the relocation. The riverboat had to fight against a strong current, so traveling only during daylight hours and averaging five miles per hour with a stop in Matamoros, the boat trip likely took four days. On average, a marching army covers fifteen miles daily, so the land march to Walnut Springs would take at least ten days. These two segments combine to a total of two weeks or more.

They were only six miles from Walnut Springs when the columns suddenly stopped. A dispatch arrived from headquarters, and the colonel took it, read it, and reread it. His face turned bright red, and he became unsteady in his saddle. He tried to read the order aloud to the men, then

---

1. Wallace, *An Autobiography, Vol.1*, 123.

was overcome with emotion and gave it to a young adjutant to read. After the order was read, the men stood stunned. The order came directly from General Taylor. It directed First Indiana to turn around and return to the camp at the mouth of the Rio Grande from whence they came—390 miles. If there was animosity towards General Taylor due to the original encampment, it turned to deep-seated hatred. Most of the men would never forgive Taylor for his cruelty. The men saw it as a punishment and failed to comprehend the reason or purpose.

Some years later, during the Civil War, Lew served under General Robert Patterson, who issued the original order to march to Walnut Springs. Lew asked Patterson if he had the authority from Taylor to give the order for First Indiana to proceed to Walnut Springs. Patterson admitted he did not. When Patterson visited their camp, he became overcome with pity for the men seeing the neglect and suffering. So, he issued the order to relocate absent higher authorization.

Although Taylor had the right to issue discipline against Patterson for the original order, his return order showed an astonishing lack of sensibility and judgment. Taylor was later elected president of the United States but only lived for seventeen months in office. It was widely believed he was poisoned to death after giving speeches during an independence week celebration on July 9, 1850. However, an analysis of his remains in 2014 discounted that possibility.[2] Because of Taylor's many detractors, it was an easy conspiracy to believe. As a result of the order to return, Lieutenant Colonel Nave, in deep resentment, resigned. The slightly over 400 remaining survivors (remembering the original estimate of the regiment was 800 upon first landing on the Brazos) elected Major Henry S. Lane as Nave's replacement.

For some unexplained reason, as First Indiana was retracing their steps back to Ciudad Camargo, they were overtaken by another order from General Taylor. Colonel Drake was to send two of the regiment's companies back to the mouth of the Rio Grande, and the remainder were to be garrisoned in Matamoros with the colonel in charge. This eased the dismal morale and gave hope to all but the two companies returning to the mouth of the Rio Grande. Lew's company was to remain in Matamoros.

2. The White House, "Zachary Taylor, The 12th President of the United States," accessed January 12, 2024, https://www.whitehouse.gov/about-the-white-house/presidents/zachary-taylor/.

Upon their arrival back in Camargo, they boarded a steamboat for Matamoros. The captain estimated a four-day trip, so they were issued four-day rations. However, due to unanticipated winds and currents slowing their progress, they were only halfway to Matamoros on the fifth day and out of food. The captain put ashore, and five men were sent to forage cattle. Soon, only two men returned, announcing they had been ambushed and had left the other three behind dead. Knowing the area well, the captain figured General Carbajal had been the attacker in the nearby town of Old Reynosa. He asked the soldiers for volunteers to accompany a reprisal. Four companies quickly fell into columns, and one remained to defend the steamboat. The three dead Americans were found badly mutilated. The four companies proceeded toward the town and began an immediate assault.

Lew led Company H's charge and realized the enemy had fled after entering the town. All four companies made chase, but the fleeing Mexicans on the outer edge of town suddenly turned and sent a volley of shots at them, which flew harmlessly over their heads. The companies quickly readied sharpshooters they called "squirrel hunters" that took aim and returned a lethal volley at the fleeing Mexicans. One Mexican was killed, and four others badly wounded. The remainder of the Mexican soldiers ran away. No Americans were wounded or killed in the exchange. It was Lew's first sight of multiple enemy casualties, and, upon closer view, he felt revulsion.

The wounded Mexicans pleaded for their lives, while women from the village begged the Americans for mercy. The Americans, moved by the women's pleas, carried the wounded to their homes in town. In the meantime, Carbajal and his main force escaped. After moving the wounded, strangely to the Americans, the townspeople began cooking and feeding them. Presumably, the town's people appreciated the American's compassion. After eating, they returned to the steamboat with four fattened beeves. Lew had his first experience with a deadly military engagement, which was not how he had imagined.[3]

---

3. Wallace, *An Autobiography, Vol. 1*, 147.

Battle of Buena Vista

*In his official report, General Taylor condemned a portion of
the troops from Indiana, and in a manner so sweeping that the
reputation of the state suffered from it through a long series of
years-down, in fact, to the War of the Rebellion. And believing
myself in possession of evidence to show the judgment unjust, and
in material points officially false, it would seem a duty required of
me to correct the wrong.*

—LEW WALLACE[1]

In early February 1847, First Indiana was ordered to return to Walnut
Springs. Upon arrival, after over 1,000 miles of back-and-forth travel
over the previous two months, they were to parade past General Taylor's
headquarters tent for his viewing and inspection. As was the custom, the
officers were to salute him while passing in front of the general. However,
as Lew and his men passed, Lew only saw a rather scruffy-looking character leaning against the flagstaff. Lew thought the man most likely a
"teamster" and did not salute.[2] The next day, Lew asked his captain why
General Taylor had them parade past the headquarters tent while there
was no general. The captain immediately responded, "Yes there was

---

1. Ibid.,164.

2. During the Mexican War, a teamster was either a soldier or private citizen who cared for and drove a team of oxen, mules, or draft horses pulling wagons or artillery. They were usually rough and burly-looking characters because of the nature of their jobs and the strength required to handle the large animals and heavy equipment. They lacked military "spit and polish," as it were.

[. . .]. The man leaning against the flagstaff."[3] This didn't improve Lew's already dismal opinion of the general, with "Old Rough and Ready," as Taylor was affectionately known—appearing more rough than ready. Nevertheless, the march delivered its rewards as the men cleared a parade ground and erected an orderly camp. Fresh spring water was abundant, and a paymaster arrived so the officers could go to Monterey and have dinner, paying their bills with newly minted silver.

Shortly after, General Taylor surprised everyone in Walnut Hills by disappearing with his entire staff and abandoning the headquarters. Word eventually emerged that the general was headed southwest towards Saltillo with an escort of cavalry. It was assumed that Santa Ana was on the move toward the American army (Saltillo is about eight miles north of a small village called Buena Vista). A few days later, a captain from the Third Indiana Regiment arrived in Walnut Springs, riding hard and alone. He was pushing to catch up with his regiment that had already arrived in Saltillo. He asked for someone to accompany him on the remainder of his ride, and Lew somehow got himself chosen. Within thirty minutes, he had found a rideable mustang, sufficient riding tack, and a double-barrel shotgun.

They were again riding hard with the captain carrying their lunch and Lew the shotgun. It took two days to reach Saltillo, after which they learned the two armies had gathered against each other near Buena Vista, so they proceeded south to join the engagement. But it was now the evening of February 24, and they were too late. The battle was over, and the Mexican Army had retreated. The Americans had been able to fight their way to a stalemate. Santa Ana had reasoned withdrawing under the cloak of darkness was the better part of valor. Although General Taylor was the commanding officer and politically touted as the "Hero of Buena Vista," it was Colonel Jefferson Davis whom military experts lauded for the relative success of the battle. Davis's tactics created an advantage for the outmanned Americans on the second and deciding day that Santa Ana could not overcome.

February 22, 1847, had been the first day of the battle; the morning hours had only created minor and brief skirmishes because Santa Ana's

---

3. Wallace, *An Autobiography, Vol. 1*, 154.

men had just finished an exhausting sixty-mile march and were not yet in position. Santa Ana had been wise in his choice of geography. Buena Vista had towering mountains on both sides with a narrow passage between them. The end of the narrows rose into a plateau. The Mexican General had placed his main force on the plateau, giving him the high-ground advantage. He put one division on his left to attack down the main road to the narrows, and two more divisions were readied to charge from the plateau in an east-to-west oblique attack on United States General Hill's left. He also deployed some light artillery to the high mountain area east of the plateau. It was formidable positioning and a solid battle plan designed to surprise and confuse.

Hostilities began in earnest at 3:00 P.M. with the exchange of fire between the Mexicans coming down the main road and the Americans in the narrows. The firefight went on until nightfall. By the end of the day, the leading American force had withdrawn to the base of a mountain. But the Second Indiana and Second Illinois Regiments had scaled the plateau and maintained their position to engage Santa Ana. They stayed on equal ground should the next day's attack come from that direction. Taylor thought the day had seen sufficient progress and returned to Saltillo to look to his rear and supply line defense.

That night was bitterly cold and windy, with a constant drizzle in the battle area. By early morning on February 23, both sides were agitated and anxious. The Americans probably more so, as they were now aware they were vastly outnumbered (about three to one). Santa Ana began the day with a simultaneous attack on the narrows and the American's position on the plateau. An American artillery battery and the First Illinois Regiment easily repulsed the narrows attack. Earlier that morning, the Arkansas and Kentucky cavalry had scaled the plateau to support the Second Indiana and First Illinois Regiments. However, when the Mexican attack began on the plateau, both cavalry units broke up in confusion. Second Indiana and First Illinois were attacked by a superior enemy force without effective cavalry support.

The fighting on the plateau became heavy and fierce—likely due to the onslaught and also the mistake of thinking the artillery had retreated, Colonel William A. Bowles (an important name that will reappear later in this book) of Second Indiana gave an order to, "Stop firing and re-treat."[4] His soldiers responded post-haste; some would claim too hastily. General Taylor did not return to the battlefield until around 9:00 A.M. By then, things had significantly deteriorated for the Americans, and General Wool told Taylor he felt they were defeated. To his credit, Taylor responded he believed that was for him to decide.

General Taylor ordered Jefferson Davis and his Mississippi Rifles (who had accompanied him back and forth to Saltillo) to rally Second Indiana while ordering Third Indiana to reinforce Davis. As a result, Davis began a counterattack on the plateau. At first, he could only hold his position but later moved forward with the help of Taylor's "flying artillery," which began to rip holes in the Mexican ranks.[5] Santa Ana moved up a battery of sixteen-pounders, but they were too slow and inaccurate to overcome the opposing firepower and advance. During the exchange, Santa Ana had a horse shot out from underneath him, which undoubtedly rattled his psyche and undermined his confidence. However, by the end of this first phase of the battle, Santa Ana had partially collapsed Taylor's left, decimated the Arkansas and Kentucky cavalry, severely weakened the Second Indiana Regiment and maintained his plateau position.

Taylor sustained heavy losses but still had an effective force and held his position. Seeing Taylor's left folded, Santa Ana sent an uncommit-ted division to collapse Taylor's extreme left completely. Again, to his credit, Taylor saw the movement of the Mexican division and sent the Mississippi Rifles, the Third Indiana Regiment, and Bragg's artillery to confront them. Taylor's deployment was soon in place, and at seven-ty yards from the oncoming Mexicans, the Americans let loose with a well-coordinated volley of muskets and canisters.[6] The Mexican division crumpled in piles of bodies. The Mississippians rushed the Mexicans brandishing eighteen-inch bowie knives, viciously ending the lives of the wounded, while Third Indiana pursued the remaining combatants into

---

4. Ibid., 171.

5. Using cannons pulled by horse teams to increase their mobility and effectiveness was known as flying artillery. A strategy that was new to the Mexicans, it was used against them with devastating effectiveness.

6. A canister consisted of a closed metal cylinder typically loosely filled with iron balls packed with sawdust to add solidity and cohesion to the mass and prevent the balls from crowding each other when the round was fired. When fired, the canister disintegrates, and its shards and projectiles spread out in a conical formation, causing a wide swath of destruction (usually used at distances under 400 yards).

a nearby ravine. A severe thunderstorm suddenly hit, and the Mexicans took this opportunity to put up a false white flag distraction, which allowed them to escape the ravine. Otherwise, their entire division might have been massacred by the Americans.

Although Taylor had held the field, his army was depleted and exhausted. The only regiment that hadn't turned its back on the enemy that day was Jefferson Davis's, and Taylor once again asked Davis to accompany him back to Saltillo. Taylor intended to leave Davis to garrison Saltillo while returning to Buena Vista the following day with six companies from Illinois and some additional Mississippi infantry. His forces would then return to their original strength. Two entire regiments made it to Buena Vista on the night of February 23. In addition, forty supply wagons arrived early the following morning in Saltillo, much to Taylor's relief. As the sun rose above the mountains in Buena Vista on February 24, the Americans realized Santa Ana had kept his campfires burning all night as a deception for an overnight withdrawal. The Mexican general didn't think he had enough supplies to sustain another day of fighting and had no option but to retreat. He withdrew back to Agua Nueva to re-supply and hopefully lure Taylor into an open-ground confrontation, but Taylor didn't take the bait. The Battle of Buena Vista was essentially over, and Lew arrived too late to participate.

Even though only Jefferson Davis and First Mississippi had not retreated from the enemy at some point, Taylor's official report concerning the battle on February 23 denounced the Second Indiana Regiment for its rapid retreat on the plateau. Taylor then returned to Monterey and would never face the Mexican army again. Lew would never forget the Battle of Buena Vista nor forgive Taylor for criticizing Second Indiana. After talking with observers and participants, he would contend first that Bowles had given a shameful order, but in the face of overwhelming odds. Second, Bowles realized his cavalry support was in chaos. Third, Bowles believed that Bragg's artillery had retreated. Fourth, after his retreat, despite heavy losses, Bowles and other Indiana officers were able to rally 150-200 men from Second Indiana, stayed on the battlefield the remainder of the day, and effectively supported Colonel Davis during his counterattack. Two military court inquiries into Second Indiana's performance backed Lew's opinion, yet Taylor refused to change his report. The official aggregate numbers for Second Indiana were thirty-two dead, seventy-one wounded, and four missing. Their losses in the two-day battle were second only to Second Illinois, with forty-eight dead, seventy-five wounded, and three missing. Lew would never acknowledge any truth or justification in Taylor's report.

Historical estimates vary widely and are difficult to cite, but Taylor overall lost approximately 2,000 of his fighting force of 5,000 leading up to and by the end of the second day at Buena Vista. Santa Ana also suffered an estimated 2,000 losses out of his original number of about 14,000.[7] Lew would comment many years later about Taylor; "[. . .] a man may have been a successful general and popular president of the United States, yet lack the elements without which no one can be truly great—justice and truth."[8]

7. Amy Tikkanen, "Battle of Buena Vista," Britanica Online Encyclopedia, accessed January 2, 2024, https://www.britannica.com/event/Battle-of-Buena-Vista.

8. Wallace, *An Autobiography, Vol. 1*, 192.

Battallón de San Patricio

As a result of some of the passionate opposition to the Mexican-American War, a rare historical phenomenon occurred within the ranks of the United States Army, manifesting itself by some US soldiers changing sides before and during the hostilities. The story illustrates the fractured social and political conflicts within the United States and its military. It also provides another perspective to question Lew Wallace's support of the war.

John Riley, an Irish-Catholic immigrant who once trained West Point cadets in artillery, is considered a national hero in Mexico. In the United States, however, he is a deserter and traitor. In 1846, Riley was dispatched to the disputed Mexican-United States border area just before the declaration of war. He arrived at the Rio Grande but didn't stop there, proceeding further south until he crossed into Mexico and offered his services and expertise to the Mexican Army. They accepted and made him the leader of a battalion numbering approximately 200 United States volunteers. His recruits weren't all Irish but predominantly Catholics from various European countries who opposed the Mexican-American War. The Mexicans were mostly Catholic—thus, the battalion was named *El Battallón de San Patricio* or "St. Patrick's Battalion." Their opposition was rooted in the fact they were primarily poor immigrants who shared a religious bond. Since arriving in the United States, they had faced considerable racial and religious prejudice, like we still see in the United States today, albeit against different races and religions.

At that time, most American military officers were Protestant, and descendants of such lineage were generally assumed to be nativists.[1] They considered European immigrants ignorant "papist" foreigners who pledged their allegiance first to the pope in Rome, not the United States.[2] Regardless of the reasons, these officers treated Catholic-immigrant soldiers more harshly. Since approximately 40 percent of all American troops were immigrants, General Santa Anna of Mexico tried to capitalize on the dissensions in the United States ranks by offering incentives like money and land to all who joined the Mexican cause. The incentives undoubtedly induced some to flip to the Mexican side, but many historians believe European Catholics were moved by their dismal treatment, combined with the cause of the Mexican people, who they saw as being terrorized by an imperialistic government like the ones they had crossed an ocean to escape.

John Riley survived the Mexican-American War, but many of his cohorts did not. In one instance at the Battle of Churubusco, where many observed and lauded the *San Patricios* for fighting bravely and effectively against US troops, about seventy-five members were forced to surrender. The commanding US general, Winfield Scott, ordered nothing short of blatant revenge on the captives, and his punishments included floggings, human brandings, and hangings. Riley escaped the noose on a technicality that he deserted before the proclamation of war had passed. Still, he was whipped and face-branded in a singular, brutal, public display.

Scott then set aside a group of the *San Patricios* to be hung together in what can only be described as a "theatrical process," to be carried out immediately after the walls of the Chapultepec Castle in Mexico City (manned by many young Mexican cadets) was breached, and the American flag hoisted.[3] The men were not allowed a hood or blindfold. Instead, they were individually bound and noosed, stood shoulder to

---

1. The meaning of nativist supports the policy of protecting the interests of the native-born against those of immigrants. Sometimes, they are also known as advocates for the theory that concepts, mental capacities, and mental structures are innate rather than acquired by learning.

2. A papist is a term or an anti-Catholic slur referring to the Roman Catholic Church, its teachings, practices, or adherents. The term was coined during the English Reformation to denote a person loyal to the pope rather than the Church of England.

3. Regular Mexican troops and young cadets from the Mexican military academy defended Chapultepec Castle. The estimated number of cadets at the attack ranges from 50 to 200. After two hours of fighting, the Mexican commander ordered a retreat. However, legend has it that six cadets refused the order and kept fighting, and the last of the six left alive, Juan Escutia, leaped from the Castle walls wrapped in the Mexican Flag to prevent it from being captured.

shoulder along a scaffolding with a clear view of the castle, then forced to watch the attack. They were told when the command to hang them in unison would be given. After a few hours of standing in this manner, Chapultepec Castle was taken, the flag raised, and the order given.[4]

The only thing this dramatic mass execution accomplished was solidifying the immigrant soldier's opinion of United States officers as racist bigots, undermining the army's ability to control volunteer troops while occupying the Mexican capital.

---

4. Francine Uenuma, "During the Mexican-American War, Irish-Americans Fought for Mexico in the 'Saint Battalion,'" Smithsonian.com, March 15, 2019, accessed October 10, 2023, https://www.smithsonianmag.com/history/mexican-american-war-irish-immigrants-deserted-us-army-fight-against-america-180971713/.

Treaty

Eventually, 11,500 American troops died of either battle wounds or illness during the Mexico campaign, as well as many thousands of Mexican troops and innocent civilians.[1] The documented and undocumented atrocities wrought upon the Mexican public by mostly undisciplined volunteer US soldiers could fill a book of its own. First, however, there were numerous stories of Mexican troops mutilating American soldiers, which undoubtedly instigated some misguided retribution on Mexican civilians.[2] But then there's the indiscriminate shelling of the general population by a frustrated Winfield Scott in Veracruz, killing at least 500 noncombatants, naming only one incident documented by foreign correspondents in the city. Finally, the Mexican-American War ended with the signing of the Treaty of Guadalupe Hidalgo in early 1848 by Nicholas Trist, chief clerk to Secretary of State James Buchanan.

Trist was an unlikely and curious choice as chief negotiator. His only obvious qualification was that he had been a controversial US counsel to Cuba and spoke Spanish (if you didn't know, he was also married to Thomas Jefferson's granddaughter). Even more contentious, Trist had received an immediate recall order from President Polk, which he blatantly ignored before signing. Some historians believe Trist ignored Polk

---

1. Adam Zeidan, "Mexican-American War," Britannica Online Encyclopedia, accessed September 2, 2023, https://www.britannica.com/event/Mexican-American-War.

2. US Regulars wore primarily green uniforms during the Mexican War. The War exacerbated both countries' poor opinions of one another. The Mexican word *gringo* (originally meant to be derogatory) was coined around this period by combining the English words words "green and go."

to prevent further atrocities, and some believe it was to help save Scott's proverbial bacon. Scott was down to fewer than 5,000 effective troops and was constantly cut off from his extended supply line by a tenacious and relentless Mexican insurgency. Scott's ability to survive the occupation of the Mexican capital was becoming a significant concern. Either way, Polk was furious, except when he received the treaty, he realized Trist had secured Texas, New Mexico, and California and leveraged Arizona, western Colorado, Utah, and Nevada for half the original price. Polk submitted the treaty to the Senate for ratification, which was passed by a vote of 34-14. On Trist's return to Washington, Polk promptly fired him and denied any salary payments earned during treaty negotiations. Twenty-two years later, after being named postmaster of Alexandria, VA, he was awarded all his back pay during the Grant presidential administration.

On the upside, what started as a border dispute between the Nueces River (Mexican claim) and the Rio Grande (US claim) ended in the United States obtaining all the land now covered by New Mexico, Utah, Nevada, Arizona, California, Texas, and western Colorado, for the "negotiated price" of $15 million, thereby gaining over 500,000 square miles of new territory. On the downside, it boosted the image of the United States as an imperialistic thug, particularly in the eyes of European powers. This European perception would haunt The Union during the American Civil War only thirteen years later when France and England remained neutral in the conflict and offered no formal assistance to either side. However, some elitists in France provided back-door financial assistance to the Confederacy.

In modern times, with the benefit of 175 years of reflection, the Mexican-American War is not a war often discussed in social, political, or military circles. It is considered a dark and forgettable period of United States history. Lew Wallace always refused to view it in that manner. However, some historians have questioned whether he later supported the Mexican-American War or wanted to contradict Ulysses S. Grant. Grant became a significant detractor of Wallace during the Civil War. The more revealing questions are: did Lew Wallace ever question any war the United States fought before or during his lifetime? Was any reason to partake in the pageantry and excitement of war sufficient for him?

Returning Home

*I have never regretted the year left behind me as a soldier in
Mexico; neither have I at any time since been troubled with a
qualm about the propriety even to the righteousness of the War.
Saying nothing about the glory won, our country has been in
every respect greater and better of its consequences.*

—Lew Wallace[1]

On May 24, 1847, First Indiana left Walnut Springs. There were no
significant engagements since Lew's return from Buena Vista in late
February. Their enlistment was over, and they headed home. However,
upon returning to the mouth of the Rio Grande, they met a frightful
sight: several buried bodies had resurfaced, this time in the form of skel-
etons. All the horrors of the previous year had come back to haunt them
by an unearthed cemetery.

Lew commented later that the sheer number of them was shock-
ing, and a working party was quickly gathered to rebury the exposed
remains.[2] Shortly after, they boarded a brig and headed for New Orleans,
where they received a lukewarm reception. Lew and his fellow soldiers
soon learned that the Mexican-American War had been discussed with
extreme bitterness over the previous year, and at least half the inhabitants

1. Wallace, *An Autobiography, Vol. 1*, 195.
2. Ibid., 193.

of New Orleans viewed it as an "unholy invasion." Nevertheless, a celebration was organized in the main square, but it was anything but jubilant. First Indiana was anxious to board a riverboat home, and they were soon on their way.

A few weeks later, Lew was back in his father's law office, mixing pettifogging with law studies. But he got sidetracked supporting Henry Clay's 1848 effort to win the Whig nomination for President. He was disappointed when the nomination went to Zachary Taylor over Clay, Daniel Webster, and Winfield Scott on the fourth ballot. So disappointed, Lew left the Whig party to become a staunch Democrat. He also concluded it was time to focus on getting his law license, but it wouldn't be long before another distraction would enter his life.

Lew received an invitation to attend the 1848 Wabash College Commencement in Crawfordsville. Among those entertaining a reception was Mrs. Henry S. Lane, wife of the First Indiana Regiment lieutenant colonel and second daughter of Major Isaac C. Elston, a wealthy real estate developer in town. At the reception, Lew had the pleasure of meeting Major Elston's third daughter, Susan. She had just graduated from a Quaker school for girls in Poughkeepsie, New York. Just eighteen years old, Lew recalled Susan had the modest bearing of a veiled nun. Not exactly a dreamy image, but he immediately fell in love and remarked that she was beautiful in his eyes.[3] One might imagine what Lew immediately recognized was an intelligent and gentle soul with tolerance and emotional strength. He also likely understood a woman would need these qualities to balance his self-proclaimed ambitions and fiery temperament. From that day, the courtship began and progressed to lifelong success.

Not long after meeting Susan, Lew applied to take the state bar exam in Indianapolis. Three or four days after the exam, he received an official envelope addressed to "Lewis Wallace, Esquire, Attorney-at-Law." There were two enclosures: Lew's state law license and a personal note from Judge Isaac Blackford, which read, "Permit me to congratulate you upon your safe return from Mexico."[4]

3. Ibid., 208.
4. Ibid., 212–13.

Back to the Wabash

Lew now had to consider where to best use his newly acquired law license. He immediately ruled out Indianapolis, thinking his youth and years as a pettifogger might render him disrespect among the older local bar members, and it was fifty miles from Susan. Crawfordsville was possible, but Lew feared hanging his shingle in "Elston Town" (as Lew referred to it) might appear he was seeking favor with Susan's father. He had family and friends in Covington, a growing town only twenty-nine miles from Crawfordsville on a good road. Covington was Lew's choice, and after moving and nailing his shingle to his new office door, he took inventory of his working capital. It was a $1.75 total; the dollar was a paper note issued by a bank that had just failed. But the local hotel and landlord were patient, and soon, a few clients hired him. One day, the county clerk, Judge Joseph Ristine, stopped Lew on the street and offered him work in court making records. It helped ease his financial strain and gave him visibility at the courthouse.

Around that same time, Judge Ristine ran for the Constitutional Convention, and Lew publicly supported him as a Democratic candidate. Another local attorney, also running for the convention, made disparaging remarks about Lew supporting Ristine that appeared in the local newspaper. Lew was incensed and immediately began to plan his revenge. Lew and the local sheriff were good friends, so Lew put the sheriff up to call him to speak at the next public campaign event immediately after the offending attorney gave his speech. The day came, the offending attorney finished his speech, Lew's name was called, and he rose to speak. The offending attorney grabbed Lew's arm, claiming he was not a candidate and could not speak. Lew immediately punched him, and the attorney fell towards some other men, one being the local justice of the peace, Dempsey Glasscock. Lew was charged with assault and battery and was put on trial before Glasscock.

"Guilty or not guilty?" Glasscock barked.

"Guilty!" Lew barked back.[1]

The crowd voiced their support for Lew. Glasscock quieted the crowd, fined Lew $5.00, and ordered him to hand his hat to the sheriff. He directed the sheriff to collect the fine from Lew's apparent supporters in the crowd, which he did. The court was adjourned, and the penalty was settled. From that point on, Lew had a good stream of business. All he needed was for people to notice him, and notice they did. In those days, it was called "country-style justice." Many people in rural areas likely preferred a lawyer with grit, willing to deliver a punch when personal honor demanded it.

One day shortly thereafter, Lew was invited to travel west from Covington to a pub across the state line in Danville, Illinois, to witness the swapping of anecdotes between five regionally known yarn spinners. Three were from Indiana and two from Illinois. One of the men immediately caught his eye and held his attention. Lew described him as one of the oddest-looking men he had ever seen. The man was exceptionally tall and had thick, coarse hair. His facial features were massive, with a long nose, protruding eyebrows, large mouth, hollow cheeks, and gray eyes. He had disproportionate arms and an odd habit of constantly crossing and uncrossing his legs. At times, it seemed he was trying to tie them in knots. Lew described his dress as misfitting, common, and unflattering, with a shirt collar lacking starch. Yet, when the man spoke, Lew was mesmerized and could not be distracted. The stories continued past midnight until the men appeared worn or devoid of stories. Then, the odd-looking man stood up and held the floor for a good while longer. At the time, Lew was convinced that most of the man's stories were a figment of his imagination. It was no wonder Lew was mesmerized,

---

1. Ibid., 291.

one imaginative man to another. Many years later, during the Civil War, while in Washington, Lew was in the presence of the odd-looking man again and immediately recognized him. He was now the president of the United States.[2]

---

2. Ibid., 222–23.

Crawfordsville

In 1850, two important things happened for Lew: first, he ran for and was elected prosecuting attorney in Covington, and with that came a steady and respectable income. Shortly after, he started practicing the concept of journaling grand jury testimony and having the witnesses sign the journals. Later at trial, Lew would bring out his journal and "refresh the witnesses' memory" of their prior testimony if a witness differed from his grand jury testimony. If the witness tried to deny his original testimony, Lew reminded them of the penalties for perjury. He became a successful prosecutor using this practice, which is commonly done today.

Lew's success did not go unnoticed in Crawfordsville and the home Lew referred to as "Elston Castle." On May 6, 1852, the second significant thing happened: Lew was allowed to marry Susan, who moved with Lew to Covington. Sometime after, he was reelected prosecuting attorney, and their only child, Henry Lane Wallace, was born.

In 1853, Lew and Susan moved to Crawfordsville for what was described as "good reasons."[1] What the good reasons were are unclear, and any attempt at an explanation would be speculative. Still, one only needs to imagine the lifestyle difference between Covington and Elston Town for the young Wallace family. Now in Crawfordsville, Lew returned to the *Fair God,* putting his finishing touches on the manuscript, only to reluctantly lay it aside. He spent the next eight years practicing law while involved in state politics and serving as a state legislative

---

1. Ibid., 228.

senator for two years. He also dabbled in military study and organized a local militia in 1856, consisting of sixty-five men who called themselves the "Montgomery Guard." Crawfordsville was the county seat of Montgomery County and thus the name. Lew would have known the county was named after Major General Richard Montgomery (1738-1775). Montgomery was the first American general to be killed in the American War for Independence at the Battle of Quebec on December 31, 1775.[2]

Lew studied *Hardee's Infantry Tactics* and then read a magazine article about a foreign military group, The Algerian Zouaves of France. The Zouaves were a formidable group within Napoleon III's army. They were considered elite troops with incredible talents. Unsurprisingly, several volunteer militias around the United States adopted the Zouave style and bravado in the 1850s to mimic their fame. Lew put together a two-volume book containing the Zouave systems of drilling, down to their bayonet tactics. His company became so enamored with Zouave culture that they acquired matching outfits. They were occasionally asked to participate in statewide parades and performances. The company conducted its study and practice regularly until 1861, when a significant incident occurred in Charleston, South Carolina, and Lew Wallace's military career returned. He would not be denied significant involvement in direct military action this time.

2. American Battlefield Trust, "Richard Montgomery," accessed January 12, 2024, https://www.battlefields.org/learn/biographies/major-general-richard-montgomery

PART 3
Civil War

Fort Sumter

*Somewhat late in the afternoon of April 13th, I was addressing
a jury in the Clinton County Circuit Court when the telegraph
operator of the town came into the court-room, and he told the
judge he had a telegram for me. The judge spoke to me, and the
sheriff put into my hand a message in words very nearly these:
Sumter has been fired on. Come immediately, Oliver P. Morton.*

—LEW WALLACE[1]

In April of 1861, Oliver P. Morton was the governor of Indiana. Once
a Democrat, he was one of the original organizers of the Republican
Party. He was elected lieutenant governor on the Republican ticket, with
Henry S. Lane as governor in 1860. In early 1861, Lane was elected senator, left for Washington, and Morton became governor by succession.
Lew publicly criticized Morton when Morton left the Democratic Party
but claimed to have reconciled with him in the winter of 1860 after
attending a Democratic meeting in Indianapolis, where he was pressured
to support the position of Southern Democrats. It's doubtful Lew joined
the Republican party at that time. However, it seems plausible he pledged
his allegiance to Indiana and the Northern cause to Morton after the
Democratic meeting. Knowing Lew, his brother-in-law Henry S. Lane,
and having known Lew's father, Morton would have had little doubt

---

1. Wallace, *An Autobiography, Vol. 1*, 261.

concerning Lew's pledge of loyalty. Moreover, Lew was one of the few prominent people in Indiana at the time with military experience, and he was still young, so Morton sending a telegram to him immediately after hearing of Fort Sumter is likely.

The previous governor, Ashbel P. Willard, was elected in 1856. Born in Oneida, New York, in 1820, he went to Hamilton College and studied law for a time.[2] In 1847, he settled in New Albany, Indiana, and married a town native, Caroline Cook. Willard became politically active in the Democratic Party and, by 1852, was elected lieutenant governor. In the 1856 governor's race, he defeated Oliver P. Morton, who ran under the People's Party nomination. Shortly after his election, Willard attended a Mississippi governor's meeting where he openly supported state's rights, southern slavery, and the Fugitive Slave Law. After his trip, a fissure opened between the northern and southern Indiana Democrats. Regardless, Willard remained popular and looked likely to be reelected in 1860.

In 1859, a remarkable twist of fate undermined Willard's political career. His brother-in-law, John Cook (Caroline's brother), was arrested as an accessory to John Brown's Raid at Harper's Ferry, Virginia, and was sentenced to hang.[3] Willard pleaded with Virginia Governor Henry A. Wise to stay Cook's execution. Governor Wise suggested that Willard was behind the Harper's Ferry operation by personally commissioning it, claiming "secret intelligence" from Washington implicating him. It was blatant mendacious propaganda, but the national newspapers had a field day with the story, and Willard quickly fell from grace with both the northern and southern Democrats. John Cook was subsequently executed.

In 1860, Willard, now left with depleted political influence and unable to secure a re-nomination, supported the Democratic candidate for governor, Thomas A. Hendricks, against the Republican, Henry S. Lane. Before the election, Willard made a trip to Minnesota to try to regain his

---

2. Hamilton College is a private liberal arts college in Clinton, New York. It was founded as Hamilton-Oneida Academy in 1793 and was chartered as Hamilton College in 1812 in honor of inaugural trustee Alexander Hamilton.

3. John Brown's Raid at Harpers' Ferry was an abolitionist-supported raid on a US armory in Harpers' Ferry, Virginia. The raid was intended to inspire enslaved people to rebel. The raid failed, and ten of John Brown's men were killed. John Brown and six others were tried and hanged, and five escaped.

failing health but died there on October 4, 1860. He became the first Indiana governor to die while still in office.[4] Lane won the 1860 governor's election and was sworn in on January 14, 1861. Two days later, on January 16, he resigned after being elected to the United States Senate by the Indiana General Assembly. Lane's running mate, Lieutenant Governor Oliver P. Morton, succeeded to the Indiana governorship.[5]

John Brown's raid and Willard's subsequent political demise and death had paradoxically opened a unique opportunity for Lew Wallace, even though he was probably still a Democrat. When Lew walked into Governor Morton's office on Sunday morning, April 14, 1861, the condition of Indiana politics was in disarray, but he found himself sitting in the cat-birds seat. Morton needed as many friendly, supportive, and competent people around him as he could garner. President Lincoln had already notified Northern governors to begin recruiting six regiments of 75,000 men. Morton asked Lew to be his adjutant general.

Lew immediately recognized the offer as an opportunity to leverage the role he wanted: field commander. He agreed to start the recruitment and collection process as adjutant general if Morton would assign him one of the regiments to command. Morton reluctantly agreed. According to Lew, he went to work and fulfilled the recruitment number by the following Friday, with seventy companies to spare. It was followed by a telegrammed request to Washington to retain the overage. Lew later surmised that Indiana was the first to fulfill its recruitment quota. All of this seems unlikely, but who knows? When it came to going to war, history showed that few could out-hustle Lew Wallace to the goal. As soon as recruitment numbers were met, Morton, true to his word, appointed Lew as commander of the Eleventh Indiana Volunteer Infantry Regiment with the rank of colonel. Lew quickly set about to drill his regiment into marching and tactical shape. He had already contracted for 1,000 Zouave uniforms to be manufactured, although he claims to have significantly toned down their original "colorful flair."

---

4. Indiana Department of Administration, "Ashbel P. Willard," accessed December 30, 2023, https://www.in.gov/idoa/statehouse/notable-hoosiers-in-sculpture/ashbel-parsons-willard/.

5. Indiana Governor History, "Henry Smith Lane," accessed December 30, 2023, https://www.in.gov/governorhistory/by-year/henry-smith-lane/.

After a short training period, Lew had the men march to the Indiana State House. Next, he had them kneel and swear an oath to avenge their state comrades, whom he still believed had been unjustly accused of cowardice at the Battle of Buena Vista during the Mexican-American War. Finally, he had the regiment adopt the battle cry, "Remember Buena Vista!" The magazine *Harper's Weekly* captured the staged scene in a full-page illustration for nationwide circulation.[6] Lew Wallace's regiment of Zouaves was nationally introduced within a few weeks. In retrospect, this might not have been in Wallace's favor, as many graduates of West Point and other prominent members of the military community were still vying for positions of importance and celebrity. This non-West Point upstart was already seen stealing thunder and seeking favor. His drive for fame and glory haunted Lew during his time in the military and eventually soured him on the American institution.

6. *Harper's Weekly*, July 20, 1861, 452. Ray E. Boomhower, "Lew Wallace," Indiana Historical Society, accessed October 22, 2023, https://secure.in.gov/history/about-indiana-history-and-trivia/annual-commemorations/civil-war-150th/hoosier-voices-now/lew-wallace/.

Enemy Engagement

By June 13, 1861, Wallace had transported and pushed his Eleventh Indiana Regiment to engage the enemy. They saw their first action, surprising a small force of Confederates at Romney, Virginia, whom they routed and drove from town. After which, they received some of the earliest accolades of the War. Before Romney, few people in the East had heard of Lew Wallace. After Romney, the Northern press filled the public with news of his victory.

On June 27, Wallace dispatched a squad of thirteen men towards Frankfort, Virginia, on a reconnaissance mission to acquire an estimate of enemy strength. Instead, they ran into a group of forty-one Confederate cavalry, probably looking for a reprisal engagement. A running skirmish occurred with the Confederates, eventually reinforced by another thirty-four members, now approximately seventy-five in number, against Lew's thirteen Zouaves. They chased the Hoosiers onto a small island at the mouth of Patterson Creek, known as Kelly's Island, where they dug in and put up a tenacious and lethal defense. When the rebels gave up and retreated, thirty-one Confederate soldiers lay scattered about dead, and Wallace's men had captured seventeen enemy horses. A single Hoosier Zouave had been killed.[1] Although admittedly, Lew's men had performed with extreme bravery, beyond any level of standard expectation, in his

---

1. Online Books: Official Records, Union and Confederate Reports (Pages 134–35), "The War of the Rebellion: A compilation of the Official Records of the Union and Confederate Armies, by the United States War Department 1880," accessed December 29, 2023, https://civilwarindex.com/WV/skirmish_on_pattersons_creek.html.

report to his superior General Patterson, Lew wrote an emotionally filled, propaganda-laden report that made its way into the hands of the press.

Once again, the Northern press published articles praising Colonel Wallace and his training of the incredible Hoosier Zouaves. One would think all this would benefit Lew and his military aspirations, but in the long run, it would not; it rubbed more salt into the festering wounds of the West Point elite. Lew was what the military community called a political soldier. They perceived politicians promoting these men as a ploy to gain public favor while not considering their lack of professional training and experience. The military establishment most likely saw Wallace as an overly aggressive and reckless attention seeker and, therefore, not fit for a high command level. He was about to start dealing with a much different type of soldier, an ambitious but unpolished West Pointer who was low-key, calculating, dogged, tenacious, and often brutally insensitive. In many ways, a man like Zachary Taylor, a man whom a soldier might march past and not realize he was the commanding general. This man's name was Ulysses S. Grant.

Fort Donelson

I still think it the origin of a trouble that was to go with me through life [. . .]. Captain W. S. Hillyer, an aide to General Grant, appeared on my boat, having ridden over from Donelson [. . .] he threw a document from his pocket, saying: "Here is your report of the Donelson affair. On reading it, I saw you had omitted mention of a point of importance which I doubt you will see the propriety of inserting [. . .]. You omitted to mention that you had seen Captain Lagow (associate aide) and myself delivering orders during the fight". When Captain Hillyer returned, my mind was made up. Here is the report. It is not changed. The fact is I did not see you or Lagow during the battle, as you seem to think. Sorry not to be able to oblige you. Please return the paper to the files. Now, won't you stay and take dinner with me? He declined and disappeared.

—LEW WALLACE[1]

Lew was ordered to report to General Charles F. Smith for consultation shortly after Romney.[2] But it was essentially a personal evaluation of him by an experienced senior officer. His meeting with Smith was pleasant,

---

1. Wallace, *An Autobiography*, Vol.1, 435.
2. General Charles F. Smith was a "Soldier's Soldier." Subordinates stood in awe of him. He graduated from West Point and, by 1862, had thirty-six years of army service. Shortly after scraping his leg on a rusty rowboat near Shiloh, Smith died of Tetanus on April 25, 1862.

and he returned to his regiment content. Lew described Smith as "the best all-around officer in the regular army—a disciplinarian, stern, un- sympathetic, an ogre to volunteers, but withal a magnificent soldier of the old school of Winfield Scott—the man before me was by odds the handsomest, stateliest, most commanding I had ever seen, the one who has remained in memory my ideal of a general officer."[3]

A few days after meeting with Smith, Lew received official commu- nication from the adjutant general in Washington that a commission was on its way for promotion to brigadier-general. He immediately felt the weight and intimidation of elevated responsibility. Returning to Smith to seek his advice on whether to accept, stating "he knew nothing of a brigadier's responsibilities," Lew claims Smith reacted incredulously. But he quotes Smith as further concluding, "and I will give you the benefit of what I know about the duties of the place, be it much or little. We can always make something of a man who is willing to admit that he don't know it all".[4] General Smith then pulled down a copy of the *United States Army Regulations* from the fireplace mantel and lectured Lew on the responsibilities.

The story about General Smith was Lew portraying himself as hum- ble. There was a level of humility, but it demonstrates that Lew was still a young and relatively inexperienced soldier with doubts about himself. In the presence of someone like General Smith, he must have realized a lack of preparation for such a rapid ascent in rank, but it's also likely Lew's doubts and trepidations were short-lived. Lew had always shown self-confidence but possibly got comfortable too quickly.

The new commission arrived on September 3, 1861, and he grate- fully accepted. General Smith assigned Lew to a brigade composed of Eleventh Indiana, Eighth Missouri, Twenty-third Indiana, Battery A of Chicago, and Company I, Fourth United States Dragoons. Eighth Missouri impressed Lew, commanded by Colonel Morgan L. Smith. The regiment displayed excellent drilling discipline and had also trained in Zouave tactics. Lew described Colonel Smith as having the roughest speech of any commander he had ever met but that he possessed the

---

3. Wallace, *An Autobiography, Vol. 1*, 339.
4. Ibid., 343.

total confidence of his men due to his extraordinary persuasive talents. Lew also had a particular fondness for Battery A, Chicago Light Artillery. Not only did Lew consider them the finest and most heroic artillery battery ever to assemble, but they also added to their likability by being a conglomeration of musicians, singers, comedians, journalists, and artists of all kinds. Battery A, Chicago, would prove critical in giving Lew confidence when he advanced towards Fort Donelson contrary to orders.

In February of 1862, Confederate Fort Donelson had a commanding battery position overlooking the Cumberland River, not far from where that River merges with the Tennessee that connects to the Mississippi. With significant and powerful guns and plenty of sighting and target practice by the Confederates, getting Union riverboats and gunships safely past Fort Donelson was impossible. The Cumberland was the main transportation waterway to Nashville, Tennessee. The Union was establishing a major supply depot in Nashville to support its military objectives along the Mississippi corridor and eventually a campaign south into the heart of the Confederacy. Safe river transport from Nashville to the Mississippi was critical for the Union. Fort Donelson was an impediment that had to be taken, and the assault officially began on February 12, 1862. On February 14, Commanding General Ulysses S. Grant ordered a gunboat bombardment that ended with heavily damaged Union boats repositioning out of range. Consequently, Grant decided to organize a significant land attack to begin on the morning of the next day with the divisions of Brigadier Generals Charles F. Smith, John A. McClernand, and Lew Wallace.

Lew's brigade had become depleted because he had left his Dragoons at Heiman and Twenty-third Indiana at Fort Henry, which the Union had captured on February 6 and needed guarding. He was left with only Battery A, Eighth Missouri, and Eleventh Indiana. Grant met with Lew before the attack on February 15. Lew informed Grant of his depleted troop level (there was suspicion by Lew that Grant was aware of this before Lew informed him), after which Grant ordered Lew to send his Eighth Missouri and Eleventh Indiana to support General Smith but keep Battery A. Then, Grant handed him a list of regiments soon to arrive as reinforcements that would come together as the Third Division of the

Army of Tennessee. Lew would take command of this newly formed division when they arrived. Then Grant gave him three standing orders to follow once the new Third Division was in place: first, he should hold his position as the center of the Union line with General Charles F. Smith's troops on his left and General John A. McClernand's on his right. Second, prevent the Confederates from escaping in his direction, and third, remain in that position. By his admission, Lew wrote in his official battle report, "Under these orders, I had no authority to take the offensive."[5]

On February 15, Lew claimed that within a short period after the commencement of the battle, messages from McClernand and shouts from retreating Union soldiers made it clear McClernand was taking a beating, and the Confederates were advancing up Wynn's Ferry Road toward him. Against his specific orders, Lew decided to take the initiative and advance toward Fort Donelson and the enemy. He called up Battery A, and they began pounding out twenty ball grape canisters at first elevation and distance, 350 yards. Then he ordered the advance of the Third Division, which Lew gave full credit for aggressive action, delivering withering fire on the enemy, forcing them to retreat. Most official Confederate reports from that day claimed they repelled the Union's Third Division (failing to name or mention Lew). But Confederate General Gideon Pillow filed a conflicting report, stating he had ordered a retreat after a push by the Union's Third Division. A Union Colonel, Charles Cruft, from Lew's original brigade, also reported seeing the Confederates retreating from Battery A and the Third Division's withering fire.[6]

In 1862, the horrors of war were rarely spoken or written. But in Lew's autobiography, he recalled the numerous bodies that lay in and along Wynn's Ferry Road at the end of the day on February 15. So many that Lew's reliable and steady horse "John," whom he would ride confidently for five years during and after the War, at first balked at progressing up the road as they approached the scene. There's little doubt Battery A and the Third Division drove the rebels back towards Fort Donelson. Grant

5. Ibid., 390.
6. Colonel Charles Cruft was born in Terre Hate, Indiana, and graduated from Wabash College in 1842. At Fort Donelson, he commanded a brigade under Lew Wallace. He was wounded during the battle but kept on leading and fighting. He was also wounded at Shiloh in the head, shoulder, and left thigh when he led his regiment into the infamous "Hornet's Nest." Shortly after Shiloh, he was promoted to brigadier general and eventually to brevet grade, major general reserves on March 7, 1865, after being involved in numerous other battles and campaigns throughout the war.

could like it or not, but most likely, if not for Lew's aggressive action and advance, Grant would have lost Wynn's Ferry Road, and the rebels would have been able to escape through and turn back on the Union's positions. Instead, as it turned out, the rebels found themselves trapped and forced to surrender. They sought negotiation, but Grant earned the moniker "Unconditional Surrender Grant" (a.k.a., "U. S. Grant") when he refused to offer terms. The Confederates had no alternative and gave up Fort Donelson, without terms, on February 16.

Lew's official Fort Donelson report did not mention he had observed Captain Hillyer or Captain Lagow delivering orders on the battlefield. They were both General Grant's adjutant staff members and worked under Adjutant Captain Rawlins. A few days after the surrender, Lew was asked to add he had observed them doing so on his report upon a personal visit and request by Hillyer and Lagow at Lew's quarters. Lew asked them to allow him a day to review the report, purportedly sought advice from his staff members, and decided not to add them. Lew saw and interacted with Captain Rawlins on the Fort Donelson battlefield before ignoring Grant's specific orders not to advance. Rawlins heard Lew say he was ordering an advance, so Rawlins immediately turned and spurred his mount while exclaiming he was heading back to headquarters to report. Lew had not observed the other two adjutant captains on the battlefield and would not say he had; it ran against his grain to capitulate. He showed no practical, political, or subtle discretionary flexibility and would pay the price. As the saying goes, "The road to hell is paved with good intentions."

Professionally-trained soldiers formally learn all basic subjects at the academies. They also learn about military logistics, battle strategy, weaponry, enemy and troop psychology, world history, battle tactics, etc. These are formal training, but they also learn informally about military politics and cronyism. They learn to care for each other, cover their backs, and promote the overall esprit décor; what benefits one benefits all. This concept was likely lost on Lew, not a part of his personal or professional mentality. As a result, his refusal to supplement his report probably came off as obstinate, high-handed, and arrogant to fellow officers, especially West Point graduates. No doubt the refusal worked its way directly back to Rawlins and Grant in short order, and Lew likely became per-sona-non-grata, if not already a member. If Rawlins had known more about Lew's life, he might have looked upon him differently. But what he most likely perceived was an arrogant political soldier of high ambitions who had come from a privileged background, married into a wealthy, politically connected family, and was now seeking fame. Lew would later believe Rawlins was the principal architect of his fall from grace.

Everyone, including Smith, McClernand, Wallace, and Grant, received accolades after Fort Donelson. By mid-March 1862, they all had received promotions to major general. Lew became the youngest major general in the Union Army. McClernand was a political soldier like Lew, who also had conflicts with Grant and Rawlins, but Grant was more cautious with McClernand, who was from Illinois and had strong personal ties with Lincoln. McClernand did not report that he had seen Grant on or near the battlefield on February 15. Indeed, Lew also claimed later he had sent a request back to Grant's headquarters asking for permission to advance and received no reply. This may or may not be accurate, but it was rumored Grant had returned to a gunboat upriver during the battle. On or about March 1, word began to circulate that Major General Henry W. Halleck, commander of the Western Theatre, suspended Grant from his command and replaced him with Charles F. Smith. Reports of Grant's whereabouts during and after the battle varied, but Halleck had heard enough to warrant acting against him. A transcript of a telegram from Halleck to Major General George B. McClellan, Commanding General of the United States Army, dated March 3, 1862, reads as follows.

> *I have had no communication with General Grant for more than a week. He left his command without any authority, and went to Nashville[. . .]. It is hard to censure a successful general immediately after a victory, but I think he richly deserves it. I can get no returns, no reports, no information of any kind from him. Satisfied with his victory, he sits down and enjoys it without any regard to the future. I am worn out and tired with his neglect and inefficiency. C.F. Smith is almost the only officer equal to the emergency.*

McClellan replied:

Do not hesitate to arrest him (Grant) at once if good of the service requires it, and place C.F. Smith in command. You are at liberty to regard this as a positive order, if it will smooth the way

March 4, 1862, Halleck replied:

A rumor has reached me that since the taking of Fort Donelson, General Grant has resumed his former bad habits [. . .]. I do not deem it advisable to arrest him at present, but have placed General Smith in command of the expedition up the Tennessee. I think Smith will restore order and discipline.[7]

Halleck and Grant served together in California just before the Mexican-American War (circa 1846) with the United States expedition to the Pacific Coast. It was rumored Halleck had witnessed some of Grant's drinking episodes then. In those days, army officers were sent off to remote locations away from their families for long periods. Many officers would pass the lonely hours, finding solace in alcohol. Whether Grant was an alcoholic or not has been debated on many occasions with varying conclusions. However, Grant did seem to have the unfortunate tendency to be intoxicated in front of the wrong people. One of those who witnessed his drinking while serving at Fort Vancouver in Oregon was McClellan. McClellan, considered among the army's best and brightest, spread the question of Grant's drinking habits to an increasing number of people.[8] Thus, Halleck referred to it when he mentions Grant's "former bad habits." Legend has it that on another occasion during the Civil War, when Lincoln was again reminded of Grant's drinking episodes, Lincoln responded, "Well, find out what brand of whiskey he favors and send a barrel to all my other generals."[9]

---

7. United States War Department, *The War of the Rebellion: a Compilation of the Official Records of the Union and Confederate Armies,* Series 1, vol. 7, part 2, 279–80.

8. Editors, "Ulysses S. Grant's Lifelong Struggle with Alcohol," Historynet (last updated: June 12, 2006), https://www.historynet.com/ulysses-s-grants-lifelong-struggle-with-alcohol.

9. This quote is possibly fictitious.

Shiloh

In the struggle tomorrow we shall be fighting men of our own blood, Western men, who understand the use of firearms. The struggle will be a desperate one.

GENERAL P.G.T. BEAUREGARD,
CONFEDERATE STATES OF AMERICA, APRIL 6, 1862,
BATTLE OF SHILOH[1]

The Battle of Shiloh is considered a chaotic confrontation between two major enemy forces, but in actuality, the Confederate strategy was well-planned and executed. Still, they lost their inspirational leader, General Albert Sidney Johnston, on the first day and were severely outnumbered on the second. Shiloh has been written about in detail so many times and dissected it would be an injustice to do so here. Suffice it to say it was the largest battle of the Civil War up to that time, involving over 100,000 officers and soldiers, including many inexperienced ones. Although considered a victory for the Union, it shocked the North and South's conscience with the number of casualties it registered. The North counted 1,754 dead, 8,408 wounded, and 2,885 captured or missing. The South reported 1,728 killed, 8,012 wounded, and 959 captured or missing. In total, there were 23,746 combined casualties.[2] But to keep that num-

---

1. Edward Cunningham, *Shiloh and the Western Campaign of 1862*, (Savas Beatie; Annotated Edition June 25, 2009), 125.

2. National Portrait Gallery, Smithsonian, accessed December 29, 2023, https://npg.si.edu/blog/battle-shiloh-april-6-7-1862 .

ber in perspective, just a little over a year later, the Battle of Gettysburg would produce over 51,000 combined casualties.

Many misjudgments and mistakes were made at Shiloh by many, so few accolades were forthcoming for Union leaders after April 6. Grant—who was reinstated by Halleck shortly after his removal after Fort Donelson—and Lew Wallace received the heaviest criticisms for poor observations, intelligence, planning, communications, and troop movement. This is because Grant appeared to have underestimated the size and resolve of Confederate forces and failed to prepare fallback entrenchments. Grant presumed a constantly advancing army wouldn't require defensive positions, and this proved costly when the Union Army withdrew on April 6.

Grant was also slow in ordering troops when significant firing started shortly after dawn—most of Major General Don Carlos Buell's four divisions of the Army of the Ohio (which included Brigadier General William "Bull" Nelson's Fourth Division) also arrived on the battlefield late in the day at approximately 5:30 P.M. Brigadier Generals Benjamin M. Prentiss and W.H.L. Wallace's Divisions, through a combination of lack of awareness and much-needed withdrawal orders, were virtually surrounded by the rebels in the infamous "Hornet's Nest" and endured an estimated eight to fourteen rebel charges. General W.H.L. Wallace suffered a mortal head wound, and Prentiss was forced to surrender his remaining troops.

The next day, on April 7, Grant's army forced the Confederates to retreat to Corinth, Mississippi, but he achieved this with an overwhelming force of men and artillery (e.g., 45,000 Union soldiers versus 20,000 effective rebels). And then, Grant failed to pursue them or make a concerted effort to seek and destroy their weak and depleted forces. Many credited General Buell for taking control of the Union Army on April 7 and driving the rebels back. Brigadier General William T. Sherman was commended for his efforts by both Halleck and Grant. However, Sherman underestimated the size of the enemy forces in front of him on the first day and paid the price. Accusations of Grant's tardiness and insobriety began to resurface, and there was an outcry for his removal. When brought to the attention of President Lincoln, Lincoln reportedly responded with one of his most famous quotes concerning Grant: "I can't spare this man; he fights."[3]

Regardless, Grant reeled from the criticism. He needed to defend himself and deflect blame to protect his career. If you are a Regular Army West Point soldier, you don't deflect criticisms onto other Regular Army West Point graduates if you have other options. A political volunteer officer is a good alternative, especially if you dislike one.

Lew Wallace was criticized for failing to get his Third Division into battlefield position in support of the Union right flank on time on April 6. Several Union officers, including General Grant and Major Rawlins (promoted from captain after Fort Donelson), accused Lew of dereliction of duty for his tardiness. Lew and many others have analyzed what transpired, and efforts have yet to rewrite history completely. However, there is considerable mitigation of criticism as Lew's route to the battlefield has been analyzed and recreated. Many believe he was a victim of difficult terrain, poor communication, and circumstances, and very likely a sacrificial lamb to shift blame from an overall disastrous outcome. Regardless of fault or blame, it was Lew's responsibility to get his division in place promptly, and he was woefully late. What should have taken two to three hours ended up taking seven. The details of the march to the battlefield can get somewhat complex, so below is a simplified explanation, as the focus here is primarily on the result and its effects on Lew's Civil War career and subsequent life and reputation.

On the early morning of April 6, 1862, most of Lew Wallace's Third Division was accumulated on or around Stoney Lonesome along the Tennessee River. Lew heard firing in the distance coming from the south (Union positions) shortly after daybreak. According to Lew, at about 8:30 A.M., Grant's *Tigress* gunboat appeared and came alongside Lew's, which was secured along the bank. Grant was speaking to him on the *Tigress* hurricane deck and left Lew saying, "Hold the division ready to march in any direction."[4] Nothing happened until around 11:30 A.M. when Grant's chief-quartermaster, Captain Baxter, rode up to Lew and handed him a piece of paper.

3. The White House, "Ulysses S. Grant," accessed September 2, 2023, https://www.whitehouse.gov/about-the-white-house/presidents/ulysses-s-grant/.

4. Wallace, *An Autobiography, Vol. 1*, 461.

Lew remembered the paper as common foolscap ruled, tobacco-stained, with marks from boot heels, scrawled in pencil, and unsigned.[5] Lew recalled the words on the paper almost verbatim: "You will leave a sufficient force at Crump's Landing to guard the public property there; with the rest of the division march and form junction with the right of the army. Form line of battle at right angle with the river, and be governed by circumstances."[6]

Lew asked Baxter from whom the order came. Baxter explained that the order was given verbally to him by General Grant and that he had picked up a scrap of paper off the floor and grabbed a pencil to write it down so as not to forget the details. Later, there was a derivation of the story that the order came from Grant to Rawlins to Baxter onto the paper. It's reminiscent of the "Telephone" school game, and everyone familiar with it knows how messages can change when they pass from one person to the next. Lew said he accepted the written order from Baxter and handed it to Colonel Thayer, who apparently lost it. It was never found, and Grant stated later that he had ordered Lew to take River Road to back Sherman's position near Shiloh Church.

Lew vehemently disagreed that part of the order was given. He recollected that the route to take was not specified and that he and Brigadier General W. H. L. Wallace had determined the previous day that the shortest route to Union positions would be the Shunpike. River Road would require marching a further distance of two and three-quarter miles. But instead of immediately heading his forces out upon receiving orders, Lew gave his division a thirty-minute lunch break. The Third Division started its march at about noon, minus the Third Brigade, still in nearby Adamsville. The Third Brigade did not begin its march until approximately 2:00 P.M. Sunrise at Shiloh on Sunday, April 6, 1862, shortly after gunfire was first heard, was at 5:43 A.M. About three hours later, Grant first appeared on the *Tigress* at Stoney Lonesome, and orders would not be delivered to Lew to move towards the battlefield for another three hours. By the time Lew's Third Division started its march, almost six and a half hours had passed since sunrise.

5. For regular ruled writing paper, Foolscap paper was cut to 8 x 13 inches. The "foolscap" paper got its name from the watermark on it—a fool's cap.

6. Wallace, *An Autobiography, Vol. 1*, 463.

Lew decided to take the Shunpike route, and it proved to be difficult ground. It was muddy, and movement was slow and tiring. Finally,
around 2:30 P.M., a member of Grant's staff, William R. Rowley, arrived
pursuant to Grant's request to find out where Lew was and to inform
him the army was moving back, and the battle line had shifted northeast towards Pittsburgh Landing. Lew asked if General Grant had sent
him orders, and Rowley answered, "Yes, he wants you at Pittsburgh
Landing, and he wants you there like hell."[7] Lew realized if he kept on
the Shunpike, he'd find himself behind enemy lines. He had two choices:
move forward and fight through the enemy from the rear towards Union
positions or head back to find a crossroads that would feed south into
River Road to join with Union lines. Lew chose the latter, which was the
correct choice. However, he countermarched them instead of turning
his troops to an "about-face" to reverse their marching order.[8] Lew's best
troops led the column; he wanted them out front as they approached the
battlefield, but this cost additional time.

Lew also lost time while seeking someone to identify a good cross-
road. Lew's Third Division arrived at Pittsburgh Landing at 6:30 P.M.;
sunset was at 6:28 P.M. They could not form an organized skirmish line
until 7:00 P.M., when significant hostilities quieted soon after. Lew's
troops had traveled fourteen miles over seven hours upon their arrival.
His original justification for deciding his route was to cut the marching distance from eight and three-quarter miles, if he used River Road,
down to six using the Shunpike. His choices that day and a subsequent
political mistake concerning General Halleck later cost Lew his division
command and reputation. They also haunted him for the rest of his
life. Rawlins and Grant had undoubtedly waited for an opportunity to
pounce on Lew Wallace; Grant's vulnerable position after Shiloh and his
need to deflect, along with Lew's perceived mistakes on April 6, were critical in helping seal Lew's fate with Halleck. Halleck was also not a fan of
political soldiers and would not hesitate—when given good reason—to
thin them from his ranks.

---

7. Ibid., 468.
8. A countermarch can be very time-consuming, depending on the length of the column (not to mention lost time
if first marching away from the objective). The reverse march will not begin until the leading members of the column
marched to the rear of the column. At Shiloh, six divisions totaled 45,000. If Lew Wallace had 1/6 of the troops, that's
approximately 7,500 soldiers. If able to march in columns of four abreast, the front of the column would have to first
march past 1.875 rows of soldiers before the rear march would begin.

Criticizing Halleck

One day, however, I opened my mouth and let my opinions fly: this, too, under circumstances so discreditable to my good sense that I hesitate writing them. In fact, I would not do so were the exposure less essential to a just explanation of the evil time soon to overtake me. I make no apology for my foolishness, except the very general one that it is not in nature for any man to be always good and always wise[.]

—Lew Wallace[1]

After Shiloh, with all the adverse reports and reviews, Lew had an opportunity to save his position and status. After all, except for Buell and possibly Sherman, other generals also appeared lackluster. Lew and his Third Division fought bravely and efficiently on April 7, with Lew continually in the saddle, walking and trotting John back and forth, encouraging his division to continue firing and moving forward. Lew was no coward in battle, and no one ever suggested otherwise. He maintained the support of Governor Morton and Senator Henry S. Lane. Lane had a direct line and influence with Lincoln, but Lew continued to sabotage himself and thus hastened his downfall. Anxious to engage more fully in the next battle, he waited impatiently for things to start moving. He pondered why Grant had not pursued the Confederates to try and finalize their

---

1. Wallace, *An Autobiography, Vol 1.*, 577–78.

demise. Rumors and innuendos were circulating when, in fact, Halleck had ordered Grant to stand down and do nothing after the grueling two days of Shiloh. Soon, Lew received word that Halleck arrived to take command of the Union Army in the West, essentially relegating Grant to a figurehead. He immediately took it upon himself to visit Halleck.

Lew found Halleck appearing to be planning a move on Corinth, the next objective to eventually control the Mississippi. Halleck greeted Lew, and through the encounter and discussion, Lew left encouraged and confident he would be a significant part of a developing attack plan. He would finally attain the glory he had been seeking. But a major assault on Corinth never happened. Halleck, known as "Old Brains," eventually decided on a protracted siege of Corinth and had the troops build a series of earthworks to maximize defense and minimize casualties. Powers in Washington and the public were still reeling from the ghastly figures from Shiloh, so Halleck was no doubt feeling the pressure to achieve the eventual objective without sustaining significant losses. After a time, Lew's frustration with the siege began to boil over, and he showed outward signs of annoyance. Maybe Halleck recognized Lew's restless behavior and staged an opportunity to compromise himself. If not, it's hard to believe what happened next was a coincidence.

Three sharply dressed officers that Lew had never met knocked on his door just after arriving in camp. The gesture stroked Lew's ego, and he greeted them with kindness and offered coffee, biscuits, rye whiskey, and General Grant's favorite brand of cigars. He never bothered to ask where they were from or to whom they were attached. Later, after suspecting he may have made an error in judgment talking to them, he found out they were from Halleck's headquarters in St. Louis and members of his staff. Ironically, just before touching a lit match to one of Grant's favorite cigars, one of the officers asked Lew his impression of how the siege was going. He might as well have lit a stick of dynamite and thrown it under Lew's chair. After days of frustration, drinks of rye whiskey mixed with doses of caffeine and nicotine, Lew let loose with a barrage of criticism. As Lew later admitted, "To ridicule General Halleck's plan of operations was to ridicule the man himself; and that was what I did [. . .]. I had become a loaded car with broken brakes rushing on a down-grade."[2]

---

2. Ibid., 579.

The Confederacy abandoned Corinth on May 30. Hardly a shot was fired for weeks, except for occasional cannonades or sounds of a single sniper report. The Union inherited a skeleton of a city with nothing of value to scavenge. Lew's Third Division was ordered off to Raleigh, Tennessee, to repair and guard the Memphis & Ohio Railroad while "living from the country." Lew ignored the order insofar as "living from the country," as he disdained the practice and its effects on local populations. Instead, he had his quartermaster load a wagon train full of food and supplies and headed off with his division. Unfortunately, this was a lifetime pattern of Lew's to disobey specific orders he disagreed with, especially if he thought he could get past them. He also failed to follow other orders from Grant (who had been reinstated again by Halleck) and received Grant's ire in telegrams. However, Lew experienced one humbling and life-changing experience while in Raleigh. For the first time since the Civil War had begun, he had to view and deal with the practice of slavery in the South. Not something he would read about or hear an abolitionist describe. He saw it up close, which disgusted him and created a hatred of the institution within him.

After a few weeks, Lew received a request from Governor Morton asking for his presence in Indianapolis. Upon arrival, Lew was told Secretary of War Edwin M. Stanton had telegrammed Morton and requested Lew return to Indianapolis for recruitment duty. Essentially, Lew was stripped of his command. Although Morton would not say who initiated the move, he acquiesced to Lew's query if it was General Halleck (although about a year later, Lew found out Grant prompted it). In anger, Lew lashed out at Morton, "You have laid me on the shelf."[3] He agreed to do one round of recruitment and left the meeting with a cordial but cold demeanor towards Morton; they never returned to friendly terms. Lew finished his recruitment assignment and afterward received an order directly from Secretary Stanton to wait in Crawfordsville for further orders.

While in Crawfordsville, he learned his Third Division was dismantled. Nothing could have been more embarrassing and demeaning for a major general and someone as temperamental as Lew Wallace, except perhaps a formal court-martial. Even that might have been preferable to Lew, as he would have at least had the chance to defend himself. Unfortunately, that

3. Ibid., 590.

was denied him, and no doubt sewed added resentment. On the other hand, Grant was already relieved and reinstated twice, characteristically appearing unphased. Grant was used to the whims of political and military leadership and was an untemperamental type, which served him well throughout the Civil War. Some have speculated that Grant's sporadic alcohol abuse was more advantageous than an impediment, suggesting that occasionally putting his head in a bottle gave him a much-needed respite from all the meddling and craziness. He could reload and move forward, forgetting, or at least blurring, the madness left behind.

Cincinnati

[T]hanks of the people of this state are due, and are hereby tendered through their General Assembly, to Maj. Gen. Lew Wallace, for the signal service he has rendered to the country at large in connection with the army during the present war [. . .] the promptness, energy, and skill exhibited by him in organizing the forces, planning the defense, and executing the movement of the soldiers and citizens under his command at Cincinnati in August and September last, which prevented the rebel forces under Kirby Smith from desecrating the free soil of our noble state.

—OHIO GENERAL ASSEMBLY[1]

In August 1862, Confederate generals E. Kirby Smith and Braxton Bragg moved their armies into Kentucky. It was obvious they intended to retake the Cumberland Gap and resecure central Tennessee and Kentucky, and if successful, they would immediately threaten to invade Indiana and Ohio. In response, Governor Morton recruited and organized five Indiana regiments. He hadn't the time to designate commanding colonels, so he asked Lew to command one of the regiments now in Jeffersonville (back to where Lew's First Indiana had embarked for Mexico on riverboats in 1846). Lew viewed it as another demeaning

---

1. Ohio General Assembly Joint Resolution, OR, 52 (1): 337 March 4, 1863.

slap in the face for a major general, but to Lew's credit, he accepted it as an opportunity to get back into the fray. One regiment quickly turned into six under his command, and he soon headed toward Lexington, Kentucky, to assist Major General William "Bull" Nelson (of Shiloh) in repelling the 21,000 troops of Kirby Smith. Nelson showed no interest in Lew's help (nor him personally) and delayed Lew's movements.

Six days later, Nelson's forces clashed with Smith's, and Nelson was wounded and lost over 5,000 soldiers or over 80 percent casualties.[2] Smith was now essentially running free and having his way. Lew was ordered to proceed with his six regiments northeast directly to Cincinnati, take command of all the troops in the area, and defend the city. Around September 2, Lew arrived and proclaimed to all local newspapers that he was assuming command of Cincinnati, Covington, and Newport, with the latter two cities on the Kentucky side of the river.[3] Then he addressed the citizens, "that an active, darting, and powerful enemy threatens them with every consequence of war."[4]

The people of Cincinnati quickly realized Lew had a skill set most military leaders did not have. He applied his political organizing, legal, speaking, and soldiering skills to order, influence, and motivate soldiers, civil leadership, and the local populous. He gained the full support of the local mayor, George Hatch. The mayor didn't have to cooperate, but Lew had convinced him it was vital. Lew ordered businesses closed and all physically-able persons to report for labor duty within an hour. Rather than force military policing on locals, he put the city police in charge of maintaining compliance. Essentially, the local police became provost guards. It was a very astute decision. Locals preferred direction from their own versus the unknown. The mayor backed the decision and warned citizens that orders from the police would be strictly enforced. Lew then

---

2. Major General William "Bull" Nelson had a reputation for having a nasty temper and disposition. Despite being a Kentuckian, he joined the Union Army at the beginning of the war. However, he created animosity within the Union ranks. On September 29, 1862, at the Galt Hotel in Louisville, KY, Nelson had a physical altercation with Indiana Brigadier General Jefferson C. Davis (no relation to the Confederate President). Shortly after, Davis secured a pistol, found Nelson standing at the top of a stairway, and shot him in the chest, severing a main artery. Nelson staggered down the hall towards General Buell's room and collapsed. He lived for a short while, long enough to proclaim he had been murdered and get baptized. Davis was arrested and repeatedly questioned, but never charged. He maintained he only meant to demand an apology, and the pistol had "gone off accidentally."

3. Defending Cincinnati without controlling the opposing river cities would have significantly compromised any defensive plans.

4. Wallace, *An Autobiography, Vol. 2,* 607.

had all river ferries cease operations and declared martial law. People co-operated and went to work as ordered.[5]

By September 8, 12,000 soldiers and an estimated 60,000 volunteer civilians were guarding earthworks, forts, and long stretches of possible river crossings. Lew had commandeered sixteen riverboats and outfitted them with cannons and defensive bulwarks from stacked hay bales. He had essentially built his own little navy and continued to receive support from all types of citizens in the area. He fostered the relationships by accepting party and dinner invitations and impressing his hosts with his manners, intelligence, and grace. Everyone pitched in and did their part, from the wealthy elite to the mayor to the poorest. From Lew's first day in Cincinnati, the Confederates sent scouting parties south of Covington and Newport to observe and report on defensive activity. On or about September 12, the rebels had determined Cincinnati was too fortified to attempt an attack, and Union scouts reported substantial Confederate troop movements southwest towards Louisville. By September 14, Lew was receiving congratulatory letters and notes from volunteers.

The *Cincinnati Enquirer* wrote, "People of Cincinnati, Covington, and Newport will ever retain a grateful recollection of the services of this distinguished officer."[6] By September 17, Lew felt confident that Kirby Smith's forces had retreated, as more confirmed reports arrived, but Halleck was bound and determined to steal Lew's thunder. On September 17, Halleck ordered Lew to report to Columbus, Ohio, to organize and train paroled prisoners to fight against a Northern Indian uprising. Lew's immediate commander, Major General Horatio Wright, relayed Halleck's order first. However, Wright added congratulations on a job well done. Halleck's slight was painful, and there would never be friendly gestures between them again. But Lew's performance in Cincinnati caught people's attention in Washington, and new opportunities would present themselves.

---

5. One newspaper, the *Cincinnati Times*, did publish a critical editorial, so Lew ordered their offices closed. However, when the chief editor realized his error, he pledged his loyalty and was allowed to reopen.

6. Christopher R. Mortenson *Politician in Uniform, General Lew Wallace and the Civil War*, (University of Oklahoma Press 2019), 86.

Baltimore

[. . .] city is rebel to the core [. . .] small Union party is divided into radicals, led by U.S. Congressman Henry Davis, & conservatives headed by U.S. Senator Reverdy Johnson [. . .] authorities at Washington constantly interfere with all Lew does & he really is so harassed and walled in by political influence the poor man is nearly ready to throw up the whole thing.

—SUSAN WALLACE, JULY 1864[1]

Lew might have done too good a job in Cincinnati if such a thing is possible. In slightly less than a week, he had fortified a city of 160,000 inhabitants, discouraging an attack by E. Kirby Smith. Smith had proven to be a man not easily dissuaded. Moreover, Lew had accomplished the feat in a civil and politically sensitive environment, getting the entire city to pitch in. This was an accomplishment Abraham Lincoln himself had difficulty occasionally achieving, although Lincoln's challenges were on a much grander scale. Even so, Lew must have gotten Lincoln's attention; since the beginning of the war, Baltimore had become a hotbed of rebel sympathizers, spies, and insurgent activity—a constant source of threat and frustration for the Union. After all, Baltimore lies south of the Mason-Dixon Line.[2] Ironically, so does Washington D.C.

---

1. Richard Walsh, *Maryland A History, 1632–1974*, (Baltimore Maryland Historical Society, 1974), 380–82.
2. The Mason-Dixon Line, or Mason and Dixon Line, was originally the boundary between Maryland and Pennsylvania in the United States. In the pre-Civil War period, it was regarded with the Ohio River as the dividing line between slave states south of it and free-soil states north of it.

Much to Lew's chagrin, he received an assignment as Administrative Commander of the Middle Department, including Delaware and Eastern Maryland, and the VIII Army Corps, with headquarters in Baltimore. It was an assignment that finally matched his rank but not the field command he had hoped for. Lew was learning and maturing and accepted the assignment without issue, knowing it was a chance to redeem his reputation. Although administrative, it was strategic for the defense of Washington, D.C. Besides, Lew had learned that both Halleck and Secretary Stanton had objected to him. Lincoln dismissed their objections, which helped lessen Lew's disappointment.

One of Lew's first challenges in Baltimore was an upcoming election for delegates to a Maryland Constitutional Convention. On the convention's agenda was the abolition of slavery. Tensions were running high, and pro-slavery supporters were discrediting anti-slavery candidates, promoting pro-slavery ones, and expressing intent to intimidate voters. Lincoln needed someone who could handle the delicate situation. He counted on Lew to exercise his skills to accomplish a fair and lawful election. Lew realized to discourage pro-slavery organizers, he needed to have some show of force at the polling centers. At the same time, he feared the locals (like he had in Cincinnati) would not favor direct military policing. Besides, Lincoln and Stanton were against using armed and bayonetted troops.

Lew devised a strategy. With the support of the governor of Maryland and the governor appreciating Lew's asking for his approval, Lew gave furloughs to all Maryland citizen troops to go to their lawful polling places and vote in full uniform. They were to bring their weapons but store them at a secure, predetermined location nearby, not within sight of gathering voters. Many within the Maryland ranks complained, to which Lew responded with a general order to follow his instructions at once, and they did. The unarmed military presence worked well, without major incidents, and the election succeeded. Sixty-one emancipationists were elected compared to only thirty-five pro-slaveries. Shortly after, President Lincoln invited Lew to Washington for a personal meeting, where he expressed his gratitude. He then sent Lew to meet with Secretary Stanton, who also conveyed his appreciation. One can only imagine the level of discomfort Stanton had during the meeting and Lew's level of satisfaction.

Battle of Monocacy: A.k.a. Frederick Junction

If Early had been but one day earlier, he might have entered the capital before the arrival of the reinforcements I had sent [. . .]. General Wallace contributed on this occasion by the defeat of the troops under him, a greater benefit to the cause than often falls to the lot of a commander of an equal force to render by means of a victory.

—President Ulysses S. Grant[1]

One of Lew's biggest concerns when first arriving to command the Middle Department was the lack of troops needed to protect Baltimore and Washington effectively. Much to his alarm, most of the soldiers in his area had been assigned to join Grant's "Overland Campaign," also known as the "Wilderness Campaign."[2] Grant's objective was to capture Richmond, Virginia, the Confederate Capital. However, while Grant was busy engaging Robert E. Lee's defenses in Virginia, rebel guerilla activity increased near the Monocacy River and Frederick, Maryland, only fifty miles northwest of Washington. On or about June 9, 1864, Lew became very concerned and had to virtually beg General Halleck to allow him to gather several horses to create a company of cavalry from

---

1. Ulysses S. Grant, *Personal Memoirs of U.S. Grant. Vol. II,* (Charles L. Webster & Company 1886), 306.
2. The Overland or Wilderness Campaign started shortly after Lincoln promoted Grant to general-in-chief of the Union Army in the spring of 1864. Grant's primary objective was to advance and capture Richmond.

infantry soldiers for quicker deployment if needed. By July 3, Lew was sure an attack by Confederate Lt. General Jubal Early's approximately 20,000 troops raiding across the Shenandoah Valley was imminent, and neither city was adequately protected. Moreover, there appeared to be a disconnect in the army's chain of command; clearly, no officer was responsible for defending Washington, so Lew felt the need to act.

As was his lifelong behavior, without orders or permission from anyone, Lew deduced the most likely point to defend either city was Monocacy Junction (a.k.a. Frederick Junction), and he ordered Brigadier General Erastus Tyler and troops from the First and Third Maryland Infantry to establish defensive positions there. On July 4, Lew left to inspect the defenses while ordering his brigades in Baltimore to be pre-pared to move. Upon arrival in Fredrick, he gathered various other and sundry troops into the area, and eventually, his forces were spread along a six-mile stretch. With the size of his force (about 6,800 effectives) and his stretched line, there's little doubt even Lew expected to stop Early's advance. However, he could delay him long enough for Early's direction to be determined and long enough for additional troops to arrive for the defense of Washington. Defending Baltimore would be difficult without reinforcements, but Lew's priority was to defend Washington and, at the same time, keep open an escape route for his rag-tag army to retreat to Baltimore, where he had fortification.

At about 10:00 A.M. on July 9, Early's troops arrived at the Monocacy River, and the battle began. After eight hours of brutal fighting, Lew's troops were overwhelmed (outnumbered three to one) and retreated toward Baltimore. Lew left behind more than 1,294 dead, wounded or captured. Early had lost an estimated 700 to 1,000 men killed or wounded, but more importantly, he had lost an entire day's march and left with battle-weary troops.[3] On July 10, Early started his march again toward Washington and arrived at Fort Stevens.[4] By the time his troops reached the fort, they were utterly exhausted. Early had to wait until

---

3. The Army Historical Society, "The Battle of Monocacy 9 July 1864," accessed December 29, 2023, https://army history.org/the-battle-of-monocacy-9-july-1864/.

4. Fort Stevens guarded the northern approach to Washington, D.C., the Seventh Street Turnpike. By 1864, Fort Stevens was part of a thirty-seven-mile-long group of linked fortifications consisting of sixty-eight forts to defend the capital.

the following morning to attack. Before the first attack, the Union's VI Corps Grant had dispatched to Washington from Petersburg, reached the fort, and helped repel Early's relentless assaults over three days. By July 14, Early was down to 8,000 effective troops and observed crossing the Potomac at White's Ferry back into Virginia.

When Grant learned of Lew's loss and retreat at Monocacy, he relieved Lew of the VIII Corps but not as an administrator of the Middle Department. To do so would have been outside Grant's authority. When the powers in Washington became aware of what Lew had anticipated, organized, and accomplished to defend Washington, he was reinstated to commander of the VIII Corps. Lew's reinstatement was a public rebuke of Grant, who left Washington exposed, and many were not happy with him. Also, by this time, after the Battle of the Wilderness and Battle of Cold Harbor debacles, Grant gained a new moniker he would never outlive, "Butcher." Lew always took credit for saving Washington, and he probably did. Today, a statue honoring Lew resides in the National Statuary Hall in the United States Capitol building.

David Wallace, Lew's father

Ferry boat crossing on Wabash River

Lew Wallace in his youth

Chief Black Hawk

Lew Wallace as a young adult

Susan Wallace

Lew Wallace during the Civil War

Charles F. Smith

Ulysses S. Grant

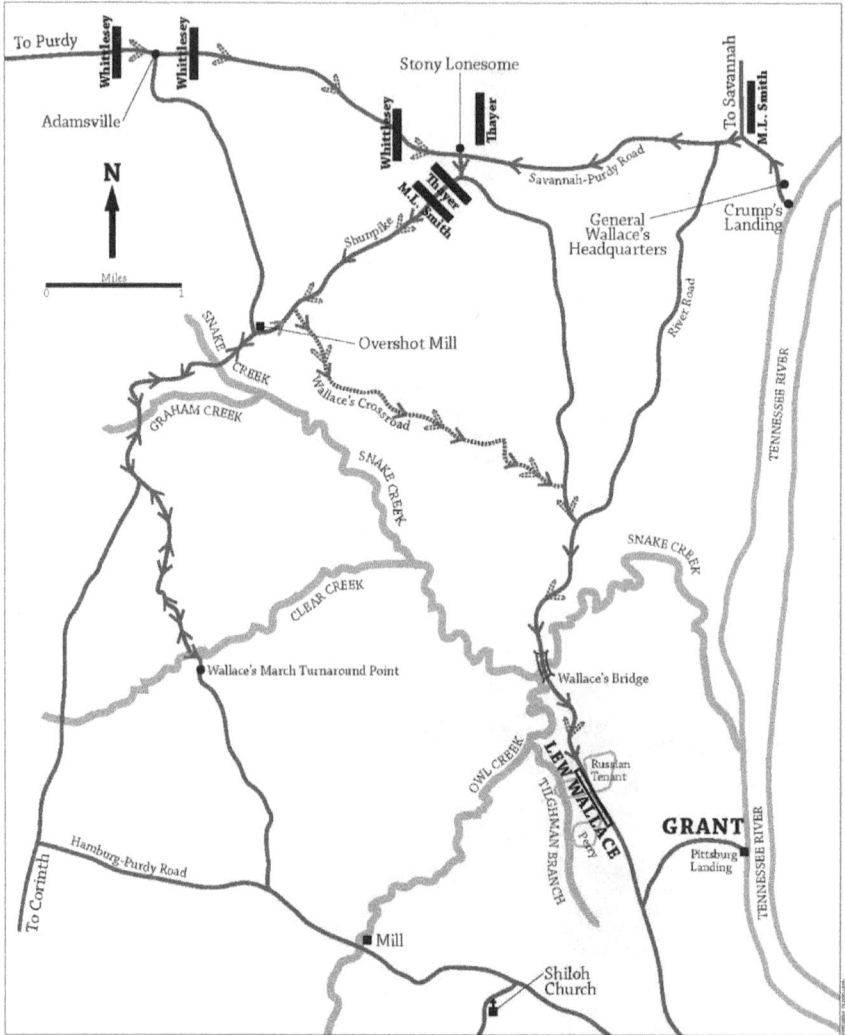

March of Lew Wallace's Division to Shiloh, April 6, 1862

Henry S. Lane

Henry Halleck

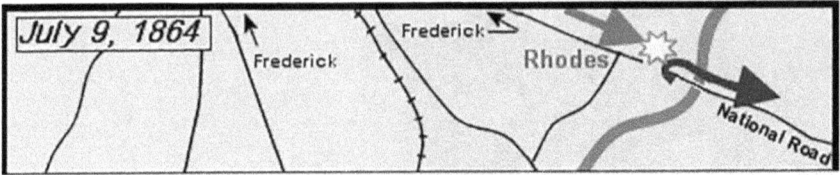

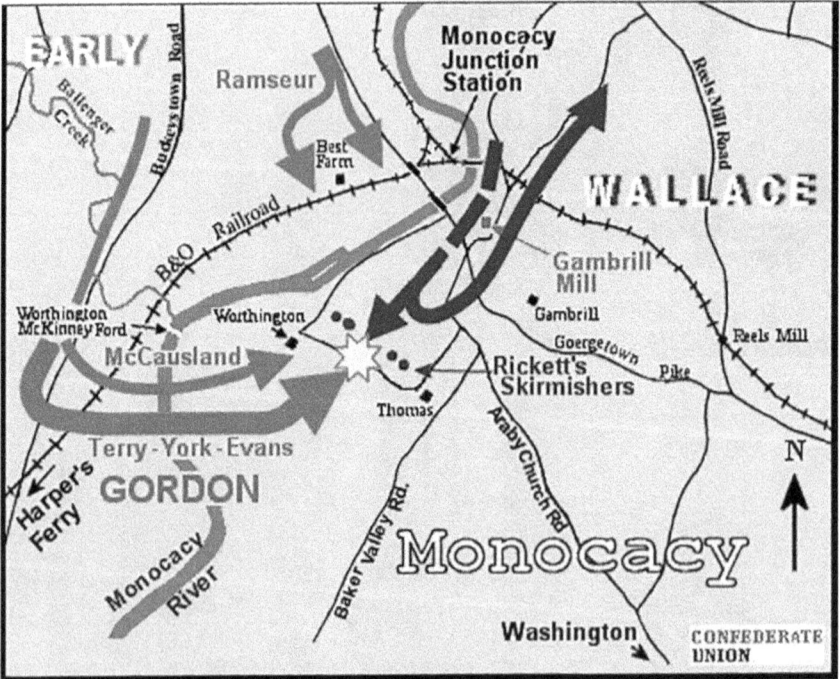

Battle of Monacacy

Lew's statue in Statutory Hall, Washington, DC

Execution of Lincoln's conspirators

Louis Weichmann

John Surratt

Andersonville

Henry Wirtz

Victorio

Lew Wallace as Governor of New Mexico

Billy the Kid and Sister Blandina Segale

Lew Wallace

Wallace, retired

Assassination Conspiracy

*While our brethren are slaughtered in hecatombs, Abraham
Lincoln coolly issues his Emancipation Proclamation, letting loose
from three to four millions of half civilized Africans to murder
their Masters and Mistresses! And all that under the pretense of
philanthropy!! Puritan hypocrisy never exhibited itself in a more
horrible and detestable attitude.*

BISHOP MARTIN J. SPALDING OF LOUISVILLE
PERSONAL DIARY, JANUARY 1, 1863[1]

On July 31, 1864, Martin J. Spalding, former Catholic bishop of
Louisville, was named the seventh archbishop of Baltimore. His family
roots started in Maryland and then Kentucky. The Spalding family were
quintessential Southerners in political and racial views, and the archbishop was no exception. It was well known that he was not a fan of Abraham
Lincoln's policies, and his Catholic Publication, the *Catholic Mirror*,
was anti-Lincoln. The paper once wrote in 1860 that Lincoln intended
to "destroy what we believe to be Southern States Rights."[2] As a result
of such rhetoric, when Lincoln rode on his train to Washington from

---

1. Carl C. Creason, "Puritan Hypocrisy and Conservative Catholicity: how Roman Catholic clergy in the border states interpreted the U.S. Civil War." (The University of Louisville, May 2016), accessed October 9, 2023, https://doi.org/10.18 297/etd/2430.

2. JSTOR, "The Catholic Press, the Bible, and Protestant Responsibility for the Civil War," accessed January 15, 2024, https://www.jstor.org/stable/26381449.

Springfield, Illinois, after the presidential election for his inauguration, the local militia had to be called out to protect the train when it passed through Baltimore. In addition, Spalding was rumored to often refer to the president in derogatory and demeaning ways. In 1863 and again in 1864, the Union's War Department arrested the editors of the *Catholic Mirror* for printing works of "treasonable character." Publication of the paper was suspended for a time on both occasions.

The controversial climate in Baltimore set the stage for a significant tragedy and controversy involving President Lincoln. At approximately 10 P.M. on April 14, 1865, a well-known actor, John Wilkes Booth, entered the rear of Lincoln's private balcony booth at Ford's Theatre in Washington and shot him in the back of the head. Mr. Lincoln succumbed to his wound about nine hours later. Around the same time Lincoln was shot, a man named Lewis Powell entered the home of Secretary of State William Seward, attacking him with a knife and leaving him in critical condition. Seward somehow survived his wounds. In addition to Seward's attack, a man named George Atzerod was assigned the same night to enter the home of Vice President Andrew Johnson and kill him. However, Atzerod lost his nerve and never attempted Johnson's assassination.

About two weeks later, after intense investigations and manhunts, ten people were identified as suspected actors and conspirators in the planning, assassination, and attempted assassinations. Six of the ten named Lincoln assassination conspirators were known Catholics. John Wilkes Booth, the Lincoln shooter, had a Catholic medal in his pocket when a Union soldier killed him, so it was speculated that he converted to Catholicism at some point before his death. Numerous rumors swirled that the pope was involved. However, other theories included the Confederacy and President Jefferson Davis. Some even suspected Vice President Johnson, Secretary Stanton, or Ulysses S. Grant were somehow behind the plot. No definitive connection outside the ten named conspirators was ever proven.

On April 15, 1865, Archbishop Spalding published an announcement in the *Catholic Mirror* concerning the assassination of Lincoln, which, although on the surface appeared appropriate, lacked sympathy and, in fact, never mentioned Lincoln by name. General James A. Hardie, then inspector general of the army and a friend of Spalding's, was alarmed by the cold tone of the article and immediately sent a dispatch to Spalding encouraging him to display signs of mourning at all Catholic buildings to avoid any reprisal or bloodshed. Spalding heeded his friend's warnings and directed clergy to display black crepe and attend official mourning ceremonies, but then he was sure to be out of town to participate in any himself.

Archbishop Spalding wasn't the only cleric to show a lack of empathy or regret towards the president's death. Some Protestant clergy, who were Southern sympathizers, also exhibited a lack of sympathy. The Baltimore City Council was incensed and passed resolutions, one of which made the following request: "that the commander of this Department be respectfully requested to close those churches named and such others as are governed by such disloyal and unpatriotic purposes."[3] The resolution was then sent to Major General Lew Wallace, commander of the Middle Department.

Lew immediately published a warning to all clergy within the Middle District dated April 19, 1865:

> *The conduct of certain clergymen in this city has, in some instances, been so positively offensive to loyal people, and in others, of such doubtful propriety, to say nothing about taste, as to have become a cause of bad feeling with many well disposed citizens [. . .]. In this state of affairs, you will undoubtedly perceive the wisdom of avoiding, on your own part, everything in the least calculated to offend the sensibilities mentioned. You will also perceive the propriety of requiring members of your congregation, male and female, who may be so unfortunate as to have been sympathizers with the rebellion, not to bring their politics into the church [. . .]. You know that what I request thus I have the power to enforce. You ought also to know that, to save the community from the dishonor and consequences of a public*

---

3. Library of Congress, "*Baltimore American*, April 25th, 1865," accessed January 15, 2024, https://www.loc.gov/item/scsm001212/.

outbreak, it would be my duty to exercise all the power I possess, without regard to persons or congregations.[4]

On or about May 6, 1865, Lew was named one of nine judges to a controversial military tribunal to determine the fate of eight alleged Lincoln conspirators.[5] The tribunal eventually led to the hanging of four defendants, one of them a local middle-aged widow of high repute. The remaining four defendants were sentenced to various prison terms. The constitutionality and competency of the tribunal proceeded under intense public scrutiny. The trial, judgments, and punishments have been debated for years and, to this day, hangs as a dark cloud over Lew's memory.

---

4. Library of Congress, "*Baltimore American*, April 21, 1865," accessed January 15, 2024, https://www.loc.gov/item/scsm001197/.

5. A tribunal is a panel of military judges, together with a judge advocate's assistance, specifying the charges against the defendant(s). The tribunal sets a trial date, commences the trial, and, at the conclusion, determines the fate of the defendant(s).

PART 4

Military Tribunals

Lincoln Conspirators

*The Tribune, World, and other journals of similar sentiments,
insist that, because the assassins of President LINCOLN were not
in the military service, the government has no right to try them
by military law. This seems to us very shallow and very absurd.
It is the nature of the crime, and not the dress of the criminal,
that determines the tribunal by which he may be tried. Suppose
a plain citizen, "not in the military service," had gone to Gen.
GRANT's headquarters in Virginia, and shot him: could he not
be tried by military law? Must he be tried before a civil court, by
a jury drawn from the neighborhood? No man in his senses would
contend for this for a single moment; yet we do not see how the
Tribune or the World could refuse to demand for him that right,
without throwing overboard the principles they now avow.*

—*THE NEW YORK TIMES*, MAY 16, 1865[1]

The above-quoted excerpt from a *New York Times* article published one
month after President Lincoln's assassination is written with passion
but, unfortunately, incorrect. The scenario described where a "plain citizen" walks into General Grant's headquarters, shoots him, and is then
tried in a civil court by a jury drawn from the neighborhood is what our

---

1. Library of Congress, "*New York Times* Archives, May 16, 1865," accessed September 2, 2023, https://www.loc.gov/item/scsm001326/.

founding fathers intended when they ratified the Fourth Amendment to the US Constitution in 1789. Nevertheless, after President Lincoln was assassinated, the Fourth Amendment did not deter succeeding President Andrew Johnson from forming a military tribunal to conduct a military trial.

The Lincoln conspirators, as they are usually referred to, were more than just a group conspiring to assassinate President Lincoln. Initially, it started as a conspiracy to kidnap Lincoln and hold him hostage. The South could then negotiate his safe return in exchange for a compromised end to the Civil War. Unfortunately, when Lee surrendered at Appomattox, the conspiracy turned more desperate. Who agreed to change it to three assassinations and who knew it had changed remains a mystery. The conspirators believed the succession of the presidency of the United States, should the acting president die in office and the vice president not survive, would revert to the secretary of state. If the secretary of state did not survive, they believed who would succeed was unclear. Assassinating all three could throw Union leadership into confusion and chaos. If successful, it would theoretically give the South a reprieve to regroup and continue to fight.

However, the conspirators were mistaken concerning in-line succession. The Presidential Succession Act of 1792, unchanged at the time, provided that after the vice president, the next official in line would be the president pro tempore (presiding officer) of the Senate and then the Speaker of the House of Representatives.[2] Regardless, because Vice President Johnson's designated attacker never mustered the courage and Secretary of State Seward survived his wounds, the succession issue never arose.

---

2. United States Senate, "Presidential Succession Act," accessed January 17, 2024, https://www.senate.gov/about/officers-staff/president-pro-tempore/presidential-succession-act.htm

Trial

*During the progress of the trial, when the proceedings were
tedious and unimportant, General Wallace employed himself
sketching in pencil the members of the commission, the distinguished spectators that thronged the court, and even the prisoners
themselves. Drawings of the latter were utilized in a picture
(painting), which is now in his study in Crawfordsville. Mrs.
Surratt does not appear in the group. General Wallace gave as a
reason for this that he saw her face but once during the trial. She
came into the court always wearing a heavy veil, which she raised
but once for identification.*

—SUSAN WALLACE[1]

After receiving an official opinion from Attorney General James Speed
that a military tribunal was legal under the circumstances, President
Johnson set a military trial date and named nine generals and colonels
as tribunal judges for eight alleged Lincoln assassination conspirators.
There was a total of ten alleged conspirators. Two were unavailable for
trial. John Surratt had fled the country, and another, John Wilkes Booth,
had been shot and killed by a Union soldier.

Brevet Colonel Horace Porter and Colonel B. Comstock, both
aides on Grant's staff, were initially named judges. However, Porter was

---

1. Wallace, *An Autobiography, Vol. 2,* (Forgotten Books 2015), 850–51.

inexplicably relieved, and Comstock, complaining openly about a tribunal versus a civil trial, was also relieved. So, a brevet colonel and brevet general were assigned in their stead. It appears General Grant wanted his staff to distance themselves from the tribunal, and Grant thereby escaped any controversy.

Brigadier General Joseph Holt was named judge advocate and recorder for the tribunal, or the court's main prosecutor and legal advisor in layperson's terms. He was also the judge advocate general of the US Army under Lincoln. It was a very conflicting assignment. Those who understood it, no doubt, pitied the man. Holt was serving as the prosecutor while at the same time ruling for both sides on proper procedure, evidence, and testimony. He could easily find himself talking and arguing with himself. Unsurprisingly, Holt didn't support the idea of a military trial. He feared the defendants would be viewed as martyrs more than criminals if tried in this manner. As for Mary Surratt, he turned out to be a prophet. Joseph Holt was a very competent and respected man. He was educated at St. Joseph's and Centre College in Kentucky. Before the war, he was a practicing lawyer and served in the Buchanan Administration.[2]

The trial began on May 9, 1865, and concluded on June 28, 1865. The prosecution had subpoenaed 422 witnesses but only examined 247. The defense subpoenaed 198 witnesses but examined 236. It ended with 4,300 pages of testimony, creating a stack of papers twenty-six inches high. Recorded arguments created an additional 700 pages.[3] Most observers believed the trial had gone badly for the accused. The defense attorneys sought many motions to exclude the judge advocate's evidence but were denied. They sought many times to enter evidence on behalf of their clients but were also denied. Some of it was due to a lack of lawyer experience. Still, most of it was because they had little evidence pointing to the defendant's innocence, like alibis and other witness denials of their presence at certain places. Most of the testimony of the defense witnesses related to the defendant's poor upbringing, lack of education, dim wits, poor eyesight, good character, strong work ethic, civil and social service, attendance at church, etc. The tribunal saw these things as irrelevant to

2. Joseph Holt Home, "Joseph Holt," accessed October 3, 2023, https://josephholthome.com/history/.

3. Editors, *Trial of the Assassins at Washington*, (T.B. Peterson & Brothers, Philadelphia, PA, 1865), accessed December 29, 2023, https://archive.org/details/trialofallegedas00unit/page/n5/mode/2up.

their guilt or innocence and quashed or ignored them. But it is also true that evidence or testimony was often denied because the tribunal had the upper hand in the proceedings.

Guilt required five tribunal votes per defendant, and the death penalty required six. All eight alleged conspirators were found guilty. Four, including Mrs. Mary Surratt, were condemned to death by hanging. The four were hung in unison on July 7, 1865, at the Old Capital Prison in Washington, DC. The remaining four were given prison terms to be served at Fort Jefferson in Dry Tortugas, Florida.[4]

4. Lincoln Conspirators.com, "May 6, 1865," accessed December 30,2023, https://lincolnconspirators.com/the-trial/may-6-1865/.

Mary Surratt

There is another thing you should know without being left to find it out experimentally: Baltimore is headquarters for a traffic in supplies for the rebel armies, the extent of which is simply incredible. It is an industry the men have nothing to do with; they know better, and leave it entirely to the women, who are cunning beyond relief, and bold on account of their sex [. . .] when the fair culprits are caught, what is to be done with them? The President always lets them off. They promise him not to do so again, and come away laughing at the 'Old Ape.' Yes, what are you to do? What can be done?

GENERAL ROBERT C. SCHENK,
FORMER COMMANDER OF THE VIII CORPS AND MIDDLE
DISTRICT TO GENERAL LEW WALLACE[1]

As to Baltimore, this simplified our task, and shortly General Schenk's sagacity was again vindicated—those working in the prohibited business were ladies who moved in the upper circles of society [. . .]. A woman in high standing socially alighted from a carriage at the Camden Street station of the Baltimore & Ohio Railroad, carrying a mysterious looking box. At the moment she was stepping into a car my chief detectives arrested her. The box being opened, there, in velvet housings, lay a sword of costly

---

1. Wallace, *An Autobiography*, Vol. 2, 875.

pattern inscribed for presentation to Colonel [. . .], a guerilla officer of Confederate renown.

—GENERAL LEW WALLACE[2]

Mrs. Surratt requested two prominent Catholic attorneys to represent her at the military trial. They both turned her down. She then solicited Senator Reverdy Johnson of Maryland, a known Southern sympathizer, to help her. He agreed but then assigned two inexperienced lawyers from his law firm, Frederick Aiken and John Clampitt, to handle the trial. Johnson showed up at the beginning phases, then quickly faded from court appearances. Ultimately, he penned a few closing arguments and had attorney Aiken read them to the court in his absence.

There were two fundamental problems with Lew Wallace serving as a military judge in the Lincoln conspirator's military trial: First, the Middle District police gathered the suspects and interrogated and incarcerated them. Lew was then named as a judge to the tribunal, although simultaneously temporarily relieved and replaced as commander of the Middle District. Regardless, this appeared to the public as a conflict of interest for the commander of the investigating district, although provisionally replaced, to serve as a trial judge.

Second, as the above quotes show, Lew was predisposed to distrust Southern sympathizing women in the district. The woman mentioned being caught with the sword is thought to be Sarah Hutchins, and the story Lew told in his autobiography is slightly different than historians have recalled.[3] However, Lew had Sarah Hutchins tried before a military tribunal, where she was fined $5,000 and sentenced to five years of hard labor. Lew sent her to Fitchburg Prison in Massachusetts, where she served her sentence without complaint or appeal. Sending women to justice before a military tribunal was common during the war, and Lew would have no reason to question Mary Surrat being subject to one. Nevertheless, as one looks at it today, even with the questionable practices under martial law, an attempt to recuse himself would have seemed

---

2. Ibid., 689.

3. Spacebattles, "For a Sword," accessed December 30, 2023, https://forums.spacebattles.com/threads/all-for-a-sword-the-military-trial-of-sarah-hutchins-for-treason.823730/.

appropriate, especially by a man many thought highly ethical. Instead, he chose to serve, apparently without question or objection, and might have deserved any criticism of prejudice he might have later attracted.

Of all the defendants, Mary Surratt would become the most controversial. She was a highly respected businesswoman in Washington who owned and operated a boarding house. Well-liked in the community, a devout Catholic, and a widow. Her hanging brought extreme criticism as the years progressed past the war. She was the first woman to be executed by the United States government.[4]

Still, contrary to popular belief, Surratt was not the first woman to be executed in the United States. There are thirty verifiable executions of women within individual states from 1778 to Mary Surratt's, and if one looks back before the American Revolution, there were over 300 verifiable cases for everything from murder, attempted murder, conspiracy to murder, witchcraft, arson, concealing a birth, burglary, and adultery. Five years before Mary Surratt's hanging, Ann Bilansky, a forty-year-old widow and Catholic housewife, was hung in St. Paul, Minnesota, for allegedly poisoning her husband with arsenic.[5] Why Mary Surratt's trial and execution remain a recurring controversial story is, in many ways, understandable. However, when put in historical perspective, while also considering the minimal federal policing and jurisdiction at the time, it is not extraordinary.

---

4. WomensHistory.org, "The First Woman Executed by the US Government," accessed December 29, 2023, https://www.womenshistory.org/articles/first-woman-executed-us-government.

5. Zac Farber, "Politics of the Past: 'Grave Doubt' couldn't stop hanging," Minnesota Lawyer, February 28, 2017, accessed October 11, 2023, https://minnlawyer.com/2017/02/28/politics-of-the-past-grave-doubts-couldnt-stop-han.

Plea for Clemency

*The undersigned members of the Military Commission detailed to
try Mary E. Surratt and others for the conspiracy and the murder
of Abraham Lincoln, late President of the United States, do respectfully pray the President, in consideration of the sex and age of
the said Mary E. Surratt, if he can upon all the facts of the case,
find it consistent with his sense of duty to the country to commute
the sentence of death to imprisonment in the penitentiary for life.*[1]

After the trial and sentencing, five of the nine tribunal judges signed an
official plea for a death sentence clemency for Mary Surratt and sent it to
President Johnson. Lew Wallace was one of the remaining four who refused to sign. The petition was drafted and sent after at least six tribunal
members agreed to the death penalty. That means at least two of the five
signatories of the clemency plea, if not more, had initially voted for the
death penalty. Many historians believe these five judges were trying to
distance themselves from public criticism by throwing it into President
Johnson's lap after the fact. Johnson was not naive and could see through
their scheme. He claimed he never saw the plea for clemency.[2]

1. Louis Weichmann Jr., *A True History of the Assassination of Abraham Lincoln and the Conspiracy of 1865*, (Alfred A. Knopf, 1975), 297.

2. Linda Wheeler, *Washington Post* July 7, 2015, "President Johnson claimed to not have seen a clemency petition for Mary Surratt," accessed December 29,2023, https://www.washingtonpost.com/news/house-divided/wp/2015/07/07/president-johnson-claimed-to-not-have-seen-a-clemency-petition-for-mary-surratt/.

Lew Wallace, true to his nature, stood firm in his decision. Just like after the Battle of Fort Donelson, Lew refused to question or change what he had already reported. Lew did not see two officers on the battlefield at Fort Donelson, so he would not be pressured into changing his report. Lew heard the evidence against Mrs. Surratt, believed she was guilty and deserved the death penalty, and he was not going to be pressured into changing his mind. As discussed before, it is an admirable trait that shows strong leadership skills but comes at a price. He paid that price, justifiably or not, for the rest of his life. Mrs. Surratt is most likely not missing from his conspirator's montage painting, which still hangs in his study because she wore a heavy veil over her face. It is more likely that her face would have been a constant reminder to Lew or too disturbing to others who would view it.

A year after the Lincoln conspirator's trial, the Supreme Court in Ex Parte Milligan made a controversial distinction between military and civil trials. The majority commented that "military law" was a misnomer. It declared military tribunals "military rule" or "martial rule," which did not apply customary laws, procedures, and rules but more arbitrary standards.[3] Since this decision, no American citizen has been tried by a military tribunal, but it came too late for Mary Surratt.

---

3. Ex Parte Milligan, 71 U.S. 2 (1866).

Louis Weichmann

I have never seen anything like his steadfastness. There he stood a young man only twenty-three years of age, strikingly handsome, intelligent, self-possessed, under the most searching cross-examination I have ever heard. He had been innocently involved in the conspirators' scheme, and although the Surratts were his personal friends, he was forced to appear and testify when subpoenaed. He realized deeply the sanctity of the oath he had taken to tell the truth, the whole truth, and nothing but the truth, and his testimony could not be confused or shaken in the slightest detail.

SUSAN WALLACE QUOTING GENERAL LEW WALLACE
ON LOUIS WEICHMANN.[1]

Louis J. Weichmann was a good friend of John Surratt's, Mary's son, and a resident at Mrs. Surratt's boarding house in Washington at the time of Lincoln's assassination. John and Weichmann first met and became close friends in 1859 at the preparatory college, St. Charles, twelve miles south of Baltimore. The institution was devoted to training young men for the Catholic ministry.[2] Both men abandoned their quest to become priests and left St. Charles College in 1862 while maintaining their close friendship and moving into Mary's boarding house. They shared the

1. Wallace, *An Autobiography, Vol. 2,* 848.
2. Weichmann, *A Ture History of the Assassination of Abraham Lincoln and the Conspiracy of 1865,* 297.

same room.[3] Weichmann, although arrested, questioned, and incarcerated for a time after Lincoln's assassination, was never charged in the conspiracy. However, he became the chief witness for the United States at the tribunal. While finishing Lew's autobiography, Susan Wallace's above-quoted writing reflects Lew Wallace's description and feelings towards Weichmann and his testimony.

Alternatively, descriptions of the chief witness vary widely from Susan's. For example, he was thought to be far from strikingly handsome. He was described as paunchy and bespeckled. His head was covered with unruly curly hair, and he spoke with a lisp. He had a boring manner that did not project intelligence or self-confidence.[4] A review of his cross-examination in the trial's transcript reads nothing like a "searching cross-examination."[5] In fact, as to Mrs. Surratt's attorneys, Aiken and Clampitt, most of the so-called searching questions were objected to and sustained. In other words, Weichmann escaped having to respond to most of them. It appears he was being protected, the court not allowing questions to get too far off track of his direct testimony. To give the court the benefit of the doubt, many of the cross-exam questions reflected the two attorneys' inexperience and lack of stature and confidence, which was unfortunate for Mrs. Surratt.

Weichmann was subpoenaed but had already agreed to testify. As far as is known, what he testified to was his decision. However, much of his testimony reads like a narrative, delivered without interruption from the official record. When Weichmann heard what happened to President Lincoln and Secretary of State Seward, along with who the suspects were, he decided to go to a local police station the following day and announce himself available for questioning. He figured suspicion would eventually turn his way, so he sought to get ahead of the game.

Regarding the sanctity of his oath, a friend he worked with, John Brophy, wrote and signed an affidavit that he delivered to the War Department after the trial and on the day of the executions. He never received an acknowledgment or reply.[6] Only seven days were be-

3. Ibid., 27.

4. Elizabeth Steger Trinidad, *Mary Surratt, An American Tragedy*, (Pelican Publishing Company, 1996), 69-70.

5. Editors, (T.B. Peterson & Brothers, Philadelphia, PA, 1865), "Trial of the Assassins at Washington," 24-28, accessed December 29, 2023, https://archive.org/details/trialofallegedas00unit/page/n5/mode/2up.

6. Guy W. Moore, *The Case of Mrs. Surratt, Her Controversial Trial and Execution for Conspiracy in the Lincoln Assassination,* (University of Oklahoma Press, 1954), 62-64.

tween the verdicts and the hangings, and two of those days fell on the weekend—immediately after the verdicts were announced on Friday afternoon.

The Washington Constitutional Union newspaper published Brophy's affidavit on July 11, 1865, four days after the executions. The paper had previously turned down publishing the affidavit because it was "too strong." Their motivation to follow through four days later was left unexplained. President Johnson would at some point acknowledge seeing the affidavit but considered it "wholly without weight." Brophy's affidavit, among other things, claimed Weichmann told him he was arrested when he went to the police and then interrogated and was threatened with death by Secretary Stanton, among others, if he didn't tell everything he knew about the conspiracy. Brophy claimed Weichmann stated he had lied under trial examination and had sworn to do so, with no specifics as to whom he swore to or what it concerned. He also stated that Weichmann told him he thought Mrs. Surratt was innocent and gave some specific examples of why he felt this was true. Brophy claimed Weichmann also told him he believed his close friend John Surratt was the conspiracy's ringleader. Unfortunately, none of Brophy's claims were ever corroborated.

Many years after moving to Anderson, Indiana, to live with family, Weichmann wrote *A True History of Abraham Lincoln's Assassination and the Conspiracy of 1865.* In 1899, three years before his death, he wrote to the Library of Congress and requested forms to file for a copyright. He never returned the forms, and he decided not to try and publish the manuscript. His family honored his wishes until 1972, when Weichmann's niece, Alma Murphy Halff, sold them to Floyd E. Risvold. The book was finally published in 1975 by Alfred A. Knopf, Inc., and edited by Risvold. As one might expect, the book is primarily self-serving, and Weichmann denies being involved in any conspiracy and deflects any guilt. For example, he writes that he assisted the police in searching for John Surratt in Montreal. John Surrat later admitted seeing Weichmann searching the streets in Montreal with police.[7] Weichmann gives an account of being questioned by Secretary of War Edwin Stanton but describes it as

---

7. Weichmann, *A True History of the Assassination of Abraham Lincoln and the Conspiracy,* 220–24.

general and benign.[8] He also admits that Stanton and other suspects and witnesses imprisoned him for some time before the trial. Still, he writes that Secretary Stanton was justified in doing so and that he and Stanton later became friends, and Stanton became his protector.[9]

For many historians and those involved today in law enforcement, criminal prosecution, and defense, Weichmann's story sounds like an amnesty agreement. As we see portrayed today in many television shows, the police believe they have enough evidence on a suspect to bring charges, but for whatever reason, they are considered a minor player or conspirator. So, they threaten charges and offer amnesty if the suspect is willing to assist, cooperate, and testify against others the police believe are the primary culprits. These types of arrangements have been a tool used for many years. In some cases, it's the only way of getting a conviction. Many serious criminals, especially organized crime members, have been convicted in this manner. If this happened with Weichmann, then to criticize what occurred would be to criticize what is a widespread practice in the United States today.

John Surratt always contended that Weichmann knew about the conspiracy and wanted to participate. However, he said Weichmann could not ride a horse and had never used a firearm. Surratt claims John Wilkes Booth nixed Weichmann from participating because Booth did not trust him. So, Surratt informed Weichmann that he could not participate. We will never know who was telling the truth, but it is hard to believe Weichmann, given his testimony about what he heard and observed and then claiming he never suspected anything sinister. Suppose Weichmann genuinely wanted to be part of the conspiracy but was excluded from participating, and he admitted to that under government interrogation (which other witnesses described as intense and threatening). In that case, it seems plausible that Weichmann was threatened while simultaneously being offered an amnesty agreement. However, it is unreasonable to conclude that everything Weichmann testified to under oath was untrue, especially when recounting what he heard and observed.

Weichmann mentions in his book that Lew Wallace became a friend like Stanton. After John Surratt's trial in 1867, Weichmann moved to

8. Ibid., 225–26.
9. Ibid., 231.

Philadelphia to work for a customs house. The belief is Weichmann was assisted politically in getting this new job. Among many others who were involved in the trial of the Lincoln conspirators, Lew Wallace wrote a note of support for Weichmann, which read:

> *Washington, November 8th, 1865*
> *Friend Weichmann: Please accept my regards and consider me as*
>   *your friend.*
> *Lew Wallace, Major General*
> *Jeffersonville Depot of*
> *Quartermaster's Department[10]*

Weichmann worked at the Philadelphia custom house until 1886, when he lost his job and moved to Anderson, Indiana. Two of his sisters and a brother-in-law had lived in Anderson for some time. His older sister Wilhelmina married Charles O'Crowley. Charles was an Anderson abstractor and notary public but was also suspected of being a surreptitious writer of local newspaper articles, using the alias "Hawkeye." Locals described Hawkeye articles as entertaining, enraging, and horrifying. Weichmann's younger sister Matilda (a.k.a. Tillie) sometimes spelled her name as Wiechman (pronounced "W-i-c-k-m-a-n"), either by specific intention or mistake. Wilhelmina dropped the Weichmann surname entirely. From 1890 US census records, Louis Weichmann, his sisters, and brother-in-law are listed as living together in the same house at 1403 West 8th Street in Anderson.[11]

After moving to Anderson, Weichmann mentions Lew's "beautiful home and study" in Crawfordsville, which one could assume he was invited to visit.[12] The apparent contacts between Lew Wallace and Weichmann long after the trial is perplexing. It is one thing to offer amnesty to a suspect for testimony that results in executions, but quite another when a tribunal judge later becomes an acquaintance. A suspect usually accepts amnesty because they are guilty to some extent. Hopefully, Lew was wholly convinced of Weichmann's innocence.

---

10. Ibid., 397.

11. Newspapers.com by Ancestry, "O'Crowley, Hawkeye and Weichmann," accessed January 12, 2024, https://www.newspapers.com/article/anderson-daily-bulletin-ocrowley-hawkey/4718454/.

12. Weichmann, *A True History of the Assassination of Abraham Lincoln and the Conspiracy,* 286.

After John Surratt was finally captured, tried, and found not guilty in 1870, he began a series of lectures surrounding the Lincoln Conspiracy. Knowing full well that under double jeopardy, he could not be retried for conspiracy or treason, he made some very incriminating statements about himself and others. He had particularly harsh words for Louis Weichmann:

> *I proclaim it here and before the world that Louis J. Weichmann was a party to the plan to abduct President Lincoln. He had been told all about it and was constantly importuning me to let him become an active member. I refused, for the simple reason that I told him that he could neither ride a horse nor shoot a pistol, which was a fact. [. . .] I have very little to say of Louis J. Weichmann. But I do pronounce him a base-born perjurer; a murderer of the meanest hue! Give me a man who can strike his victim dead, but save me from a man who, through perjury, will cause the death of an innocent person. Double murderer!!!! Hell possesses no worse fiend than a character of that kind. Away with such a character. I leave him in the pit of infamy, which he has dug for himself, a prey to the lights of his guilty conscience.*
>
> —JOHN SURRATT[13]

How did Lew Wallace receive the above statements from John Surratt five years after the trial and executions? If there was any guilt on Lew's conscience for what had happened to Mary Surratt, this could not have eased his burden. On the contrary, these statements, published nationally, cast doubts and criticisms on the tribunal members, those who had promoted Weichmann as the chief witness, and those still supporting him. Lew was all three but, until his dying day, maintained Weichmann told the truth and nothing but the truth.

---

13. Editors, "The Text of John Surratt's 1870 Lecture at Rockville, Maryland," *Washington Evening Star*, December 7, 1870, accessed September 2, 2023, https://rogerjnorton.com/Lincoln55.html.

John Surratt

For nearly two years after the assassination of Abraham Lincoln, John Surratt traveled to various countries and eluded authorities. He was in Elmira, New York, delivering messages for the Confederacy on the assassination day, and upon reading his name as a suspect in a local paper, he boarded a train to Montreal, where he was hidden by "friends" for several months.[1] United States authorities were tipped off that he was hiding in Canada and sent detectives, aided by Louis Weichmann, to search for him. Surratt stayed hidden and claimed to know nothing of his mother's plight in Washington because his friends kept newspapers from him.

Surratt boarded a ship and escaped to Europe at some point. He eventually landed at the Vatican in Rome and was hired as a papal guard. The uniforms of the papal guards at the time were those of the Algerian French Zouaves, which was sure to annoy Lew Wallace. One day, a man from Maryland visiting the Vatican recognized Surratt and alerted the local authorities. Surratt was arrested by Vatican guards and held in custody. The conspiracy of papal involvement in Lincoln's assassination reared its ugly head again, and things looked much more suspicious this time.

One morning, on a chained and guarded trip to the latrine, Surratt purportedly escaped by scaling and jumping from a wall onto rocks thirty feet below. Later, the story changed, and he happened to land in a pile of human excrement that cushioned his fall. Regardless, John Wilkes Booth

---

1. John Surratt's friends in Montreal have been thought to have been everything from Confederate Secret Service to Catholic priests.

would have admired the feat, as he only jumped twelve feet at Ford's Theatre from President Lincoln's box onto a flat wood floor stage and broke his leg. Granted, Booth caught a spur in a flag on his way down, which altered his intended landing. After Surratt's miraculous escape, he boarded a steamer bound for Egypt. Upon docking, local authorities arrested him. He was extradited to Washington, D.C., and held for trial.

Due mainly to the Ex Parte Milligan decision and the bad publicity surrounding his mother's trial, John Surratt was tried in a civil court on conspiracy to commit murder. Many of the same witnesses testified at his mother's military tribunal, including Louis Weichmann. Surratt's lawyers got some Southern sympathizers on the jury, and after a sixty-one-day trial, the jury was hopelessly deadlocked in deliberations. Authorities charged him again, but this time with treason, hoping to get some conviction. In a pre-trial motion, the charges were dismissed. The two-year statute of limitations for treason had run, and John Surratt walked out of the courtroom a free man.[2] In the aftermath, bitter debates began again and continue today.

Many still claim that the military tribunal was the proper procedure under the circumstances and during martial law. The pro-tribunal community now had the John Surratt civil trial and his subsequent release to emphasize what might have happened with the other conspirators had they been tried in a civil court. John Surratt, after all, was a self-professed Southern operative and appeared to many the main ringleader in the Lincoln conspiracy. This may be one reason Lew Wallace stuck to his original position that the tribunal was proper and Mary Surratt was guilty. Mrs. Surratt had some very damning testimony leveled at her and corroborated by people who were, by all indications, friends and admirers. Her positive defense came mainly from priests and acquaintances who testified to her good deeds and character. She is said to have made a last confession to her priest, where she swore she had nothing to do with Lincoln's murder. However, there was never any specific mention of her guilt concerning a conspiracy to kidnap Lincoln.

2. Michael Miller, "'Assassins!': A Confederate spy was accused of helping kill Abraham Lincoln. Then he vanished." *Washington Post*, April 13, 2017, accessed December 30, 2023, https://www.washingtonpost.com/news/retropolis/wp/2017/04/13/assassins-a-confederate-spy-was-accused-of-helping-kill-abraham-lincoln-then-he-vanished/.

It is possible others changed the goal, and Mrs. Surratt was unaware, but would that matter? If one conspires to kidnap someone and, through unforeseen circumstances, the kidnapped person is killed, everyone in the conspiracy becomes an accessory to some extent. It was also never mentioned that Mrs. Surratt claimed innocence for facilitating her son's spying and treason, which was also punishable by hanging.

Ex Parte Milligan

No doubt to Lew Wallace's chagrin, in 1863, William A. Bowles was charged with, among other things, "Treason by Plotting to Overthrow the Federal Government." Bowles, the reader will remember, was the commanding officer of the Second Indiana Regiment at the Battle of Buena Vista in Mexico on February 23, 1847. General Zachary Taylor had severely chastised Bowles and Second Indiana for retreating in the face of the enemy on the plateau, nearly causing the army's defeat. General Joseph Lane preferred charges of incompetency, ignorance of proper military tactics, misbehavior, and cowardice against Bowles, but Taylor refused to court-martial him. Finally, however, a court of inquiry was convened. It did not officially criticize Second Indiana, partly due to Jefferson Davis' complimenting Bowles and Second Indiana for re-grouping, rallying, and assisting his troops in a counterattack. Bowles was officially cleared of all General Lane's charges but was determined to be in "manifest want of capacity and judgment as a commander." For years after the Battle of Buena Vista, Lew Wallace had defended the Second Indiana Regiment, trying to erase the stain of cowardice. Sixteen years later, its commander is charged with treason.

Bowles was an outspoken pro-slavery advocate and a well-known Southern sympathizer. In 1863, Harrison H. Dodd, leader of the Order of Sons of Liberty (OSL) in Indiana, named Bowles a major general for one of four military districts in the state's secret society opposing the Civil War. The OSL, by most definitions, was a militia. Bowles was charged and became one of four co-defendants in a highly controversial military tribunal convening in Indianapolis on October 21, 1864. One of the four co-defendants was Lamdin P. Milligan of Huntington, Indiana, the Milligan of Ex Parte Milligan. Milligan, Bowles, and a man named Horsey were sentenced to hang. A fourth man, Humphreys, was sentenced to hard labor for the remainder of the war. On May 16, 1865, just three days before the executions, the hangings were postponed to June 2, and Horsey's sentence was commuted to life imprisonment. On May 30, 1865, Andrew Johnson commuted Bowles and Milligan's sentences to life imprisonment.[1]

Milligan appealed his conviction to the US Supreme Court, and it was overturned in 1866. As a result, Bowles and Horsey were released from prison. Humphreys, by this time, had already been released. It was another embarrassing moment for Lew Wallace, provoking people to question his opinions and decisions. Ex Parte Milligan was not only a rebuke of the use of military tribunals concerning citizens, it took place in Lew's home state, no less, and put the Second Indiana Regiment at Buena Vista under the spotlight again. The hits to Lew's reputation just kept coming. Historians have debated whether the OSL was a real operating militia or a figment of the leader Dodd's imagination. Regardless, the Supreme Court did not feel the defendants rose to the definition of "in service" as stated in the Fourth Amendment.

If one questions whether Lew Wallace closely followed or had concerns over Ex Parte Milligan, an excerpt from a letter written to his wife Susan on March 7, 1866, will suffice, "I have just come in from the Capitol, where General Butler was delivering an argument before the Supreme Court, in the case of Milligan, Bowles & Company. The room was crowded [. . .]."[2] It's interesting that Lew attended the court argument and mentioned Bowles, who was not a party to but affected by the case's outcome, as was Lew Wallace. Lew had resigned as a major general the previous year on November 4, 1865. Exactly why he was in Washington in March 1866, other than attending the Ex Parte Milligan Supreme Court argument, is unclear.

---

1. Frank L Klement., *Dark Lanterns: Secret Political Societies, Conspiracies and Treason Trials in the Civil War,* (Louisiana State University Press, 1984), 226–27.

2. Wallace, *An Autobiography, Vol. 2,* 857–58.

Andersonville

In January 1863, the Confederacy established a prison for federal captives in Andersonville, Georgia. There were various reasons for this. The South had concentrated most of their prisoners in and around Richmond, which added burdens to the surrounding area—bringing supplies to care for captives created slowdowns in deliveries on an already limited Southern transportation system. Getting sufficient goods to the area to support the general population, government infrastructure, and troops was challenging enough. Adding demand for prisoners' needs to the strained supply lines exacerbated shortages and caused prices to rise sharply. In addition, General Robert E. Lee warned the government that the prisoners would be a military liability should Richmond come under Union attack. As the war progressed, additional troops were transferred to the battle lines, which reduced the number available to guard the prisoners. In response to these issues and concerns, thousands of Union prisoners were packed into used and uncleaned livestock trains and transferred to the new Georgia prison.

Numerous books have been written over the years describing the horrible conditions and situations inside the stockade and hospital at Andersonville prison. Rather than quoting these details and stories, although it is the best way to visualize the horrid realities of their lives and deaths, it's better to summarize conditions and let the reader explore other books for greater detail. Suffice it to say that studying Andersonville's conditions will take one into a world that is hard to imagine and question the nature of humanity.

During its worst period, it is estimated that 20 to 30 dead were removed from the Andersonville compound each day and placed in mass burial sites. Most were men and boys who had slowly starved to death over weeks and months. Some died of diseases such as cholera, dysentery, and smallpox. Most had some level of scurvy. Guards shot some for crossing the "Dead Line" or other infractions.[1] Some died from infected dog bites or beatings after attempting to escape. Prisoners murdered each other for food or clothing. The conditions and suffering were so horrific that many prisoners would lie down and beg to die, sometimes taking weeks.

The prisoners had no shelter, so they used oil tarps, blankets, coats, etc., to construct a form of a tent (called "shebangs") to protect themselves from the sun. Often, they dug down into the maggot-infested sandy soil below their makeshift shelters to help them stay warm. Keeping dry from the rain was impossible. They built fires when fuel was available and cooked their food, as the food from the cookhouse was normally distributed undercooked or raw. The cornbread consisted of about 30 percent ground cobs, and the meat was usually somewhat spoiled, replete with parasites. Many groups began digging wells, hoping to find cleaner water, and some succeeded. However, the water table was seventy feet below the surface, and the prisoners mainly had small spoons and broken canteens as their only digging tools. Some consumed creek water and invariably became sick and died.

There was a hospital, but it had limited capacity and typically only admitted those in the direst condition. Few survived the hospital, which was drastically short of personnel and supplies. The men learned to care for each other and, in many cases, saved one another. However, most of the time, the sick and badly wounded were not saved. Some of the deaths resulted from severe depression and despondency. Prisoners gave up and refused to move, eat, clean themselves, and waste away. A few men walked over the Dead Line just to get shot. One man received two warning shots that did not hit him, so he screamed at the guard, "Do your job!" The

1. The dead line was mainly demarcated by a wooden rail fence surrounding the prisoners inside the main compound. Prisoners were told that crossing this line would result in being shot by the guards, and in some instances, they were.

guard obliged and shot him in the head. An estimated 45,000 prisoners entered Andersonville prison over its fourteen-plus months of operation. At least 13,000 died and are buried there.[2]

---

2. Amy Tikkanen & Editors "Andersonville," Britannica Online Encyclopedia, accessed January 3, 2024, https://www.britannica.com/place/Andersonville-Georgia.

Henry Wirz

Wirz is a singular-looking creature. He has a small head, re-
treating forehead, high on the os frontis because the hair, light
in color, is very thin, threatening him with speedy baldness;
prominent ears; small, sharp-pointed nose; mustache and beard
heavy enough to conceal the nose; mustache and beard heavy
enough to conceal the mouth and lower face, and of a dirty,
tobacco-stain color; eyes large, and of mixed blue and gray, very
restless, and of a peculiar transparency, reminding one continually
of a cat's when the animal is excited by scent of prey. In manner,
he is nervous and fully alarmed, avoids your gaze, and withers
and shrivels under the knit brows of the crowd. His complexion
is ashen and bloodless, almost blue. Altogether he was well chosen
for his awful service in the warring Confederacy.

—Major-General Lew Wallace, President,
Henry Wirz, et al., Military Tribunal.[1]

It is not easy when studying history to come across a more confounding
figure than Henry Wirz. The mutually exclusive descriptions of his demeanor and behavior are like describing a real-life "Dr. Jekyll and Mr.
Hyde." People often meet and interact with the same person and have

---

1. Wallace, *An Autobiography, Vol. 2*, 854.

different opinions. Opinions of Henry Wirz varied, and as is always the case, somewhere in between exists an accurate description of his looks, mannerisms, behavior, and deeds. One thing is sure: when people are held in captivity and experience misery, brutality, and death, they generally develop hatred for those who hold them captive. Henry Wirz was the Andersonville prison's most prominent and recognizable Confederate figure because he was responsible for the prisoner's containment and discipline. Therefore, it is predictable that most people would have a substantial negative opinion of him. In Wirz's case, most Union prisoners at Andersonville considered him a sadistic monster, while a minority thought otherwise.

Wirz was only the commanding officer over the prisoner stockade at Andersonville. It is important to distinguish that he was not the commanding officer of the entire prison. That was primarily General Richard B. Winder, who passed away from a sudden heart attack in February 1865. The prison was closed and evacuated in May 1865. As a result of Winder's passing and the reluctance of the Union to bring anyone else to trial, Wirz was forced to shoulder the responsibility for the conditions, treatment, and deaths at the prison.

When the horrors of Andersonville prison came to light in the North, there was a clamor for retribution. A military tribunal to investigate and prosecute those responsible was soon announced. Henry Wirz was arrested and charged with allegations of prisoner neglect, assault, and murder. Other parties in the Confederacy were named along with Wirz, but inexplicably, the list varied, and no one else was ever detained, arrested, or tried.[2]

2. Tikkanen & Editors, "Andersonville," https://www.britannica.com/place/Andersonville-Georgia.

Andersonville Trial

THE REBEL ASSASSINS.; Trial of Henry Wirz, the Andersonville Jailor. Meeting and Organization of the Military Court. Reading of the Charges and Specifications. He is Charged with Conspiring with Lee, Seddon and Others to Kill Union Prisoners. 'Rehearsal of the Terrible Atrocities Perpetrated at Andersonville. Defendant's Counsel Pleads Against the Jurisdiction of the court. They Plead that Wirz Should be Discharged Without Punishment. They Further Claim that he is Protected Under Johnston's Surrender.

—NEW YORK TIMES ARCHIVES, AUGUST 22, 1865

After the controversy and debacle of the Lincoln Conspirator's trial, the government promised the "Andersonville Conspiracy Trial" would be conducted more fairly. It was not. It turned out to be more illogical and confounding than the defendant himself. There was never agreement on the co-defendants. *The New York Times* article cited above lists, in addition to Wirz, "Robert E. Lee, James A. Sheldon, John H. Winder, Lucius D. Northrup, Richard B. Winder, Joseph White, W.S. Winder, B.B. Stevenson, _____ Moore, and others, unknown [. . .]." In his book, *The Tragedy of Andersonville* by NP. Chipman, judge advocate of the Wirz trial, Chipman claims the co-defendants named in the official indictment were "Henry Wirz, John H. Winder, Richard B. Winder,

Joseph White, W.S. Winder, R.R. Stevenson, and others whose names are unknown [. . .]."[1] Later, others would claim Jefferson Davis was also named. It is doubtful all the supposed co-defendants were ever correctly listed.

So began the confounding military tribunal, as only one man was ever tried, Henry Wirz. A man who was only in charge of the stockade, not the entire prison, was constantly referred to as the prison commander. It was simply untrue. The real commander had died of a heart attack, but that little detail was swept aside, and the court continued its prosecution.

Eight officers are officially listed as serving on the tribunal. Major General Lew Wallace was named president. The defendant retained more experienced attorneys than the Lincoln conspirators; Louis Shade, a local German-Catholic attorney, was his chief counsel with another experienced lawyer. After reading the charges against the defendant, the trial began with pre-trial motions by the defendant's attorneys, moving for all charges to be dropped. Lew Wallace denied all motions after a short consultation with the other judges, and the trial continued.[2]

---

1. N. P. Chipman, *The Tragedy of Andersonville*, (Self Published 1911), 32.
2. Ibid., 37.

Judgement & Execution

*The vigilance of General Wallace throughout the trial was abun-
dantly shown in the official reports. It may be guessed from a letter of the correspondent of the Boston Advertiser who, describing
his personal appearance, said that, of his striking features, the eyes
are remarkable, never seeming to sleep and never to see, and yet
whose observation nothing escapes.*

—SUSAN WALLACE[1]

*[T]he greatest judicial farce enacted since Oliver Cromwell insti-
tuted the commission to try and condemn Charles I.*

—JAMES MADISON PAGE[2]

The trial of Henry Wirz began on or about August 25, 1865, and ended
almost two months later, on October 18. Approximately one hundred
and sixty witnesses were called to testify, and over 2,301 pages of trial
transcripts were produced. Of the 150 witnesses who did testify, eighty-
two for the prosecution and sixty-eight for the defense, only fifteen
testified they had ever seen Wirz kill someone or mistreat a prisoner.
Some of the fifteen were of very questionable character. One of the star

---

1. Wallace, *An Autobiography,* Vol. 2, 852.
2. Captain James W. LaForce, "The Trial of Major Henry Wirz, A National Disgrace," (*The Army Lawyer,* Department
of the Army, Pamphlet 27-50-186 June 1988), 9.

prosecution witnesses was Felix de la Baume, who claimed to be a descendant of Lafayette of Revolutionary War fame. De la Baume testified about his captivity at Andersonville and saw Wirz shoot men. Legend has it that de le Baume dazzled the court with his detailed story. Like Louis Weichmann getting a new position at a customs house at the end of the Lincoln Conspirator's trial, de la Baume was awarded a clerk's job in a government agency for his stellar performance.

It turns out that de la Baume was not who he said he was. He was Felix Oeser, a deserter from the Seventh New York Regiment. Some members of the Seventh New York recognized him and together went to the government agency to protest. Oeser was subsequently discharged from his new job. This same situation occurred during the Lincoln Conspirator's trial, where a star witness was later identified as a deserter who testified under a false name. The problem was that Secretary Stanton always made it well known that anyone who came forward to testify on behalf of the prosecution would be rewarded.

Most of the testimony was bad for Wirz, but there was a lot of positive testimony as well. A prisoner, George Fletcher, testified that Wirz was very helpful in ridding the prison of robbing and murderous fellow prisoners. Prisoner Frederick Guscetti testified that when Wirz caught him trying to escape, he took him to the hospital, clothed, and fed him without punishment. Augustus Moesner, a parolee clerk for Wirz, said Wirz always ensured prisoners got any care packages sent to them. A Mary Dawson who visited prisoners said Wirz was always kind to her and allowed her to take in whatever provisions she wanted. Because so many prisoners were Catholic immigrants, many Catholic priests visited and tended to the prisoners. One of the longest-running and prolific visitors was Reverend Peter Whelan, who testified Wirz was always helpful and genuinely interested in the prisoner's welfare. The reverend proclaimed he had never heard of any murder or cruelty by Wirz: "[I]f it had occurred, I would have heard about it."[3]

It was generally believed in 1863 that Secretary of War Stanton ended prisoner exchanges with the Confederacy because he and General Grant felt the South had more to gain than the North. This explanation may or

---

3. Ibid., 9.

may not be accurate. Verity or not, it became the prevailing opinion of
the Union prisoners at Andersonville. The South continually campaigned
for the resumption of exchanges to no avail. Even though both Stanton
and Grant specifically acknowledged the South as having trouble clothing and feeding prisoners, even acknowledging "our boys were suffering"
as a result.[4] Then, they repeatedly refused to capitulate. Wirz allowed a
committee of four Andersonville prisoners to visit Washington on parole
to explain the conditions at Andersonville to Secretary Stanton and plead
for the North to resume exchanges. Stanton steadfastly spurned their
pleas. The four men, in turn, voluntarily returned to Andersonville out
of respect for their promise to Wirz and his gesture.

Almost to the man of all accounts ever written about Andersonville,
Secretary Stanton and his policy concerning exchanges is singled out as
one of the main culprits that led to so many Union soldiers perishing at
Andersonville. Some villainized Wirz, and some did not. Almost everyone villainized Stanton and some Grant. In retrospect, it appears clear
that Henry Wirz may have signed his death warrant by allowing the four
prisoners to go to Washington to plea for resuming exchanges. Stanton
struggled to defend himself. Wirz's gesture undoubtedly appeared to
Stanton as a political stunt to embarrass him into changing his position.

At the war's end, Wirz was a potential source of negative publicity.
Stanton was wielding the power to mitigate Wirz's threat to him and
Grant. No evidence concerning prisoner exchange policies was allowed
to be introduced at Wirz's trial. The court unanimously agreed that this
subject was irrelevant and, therefore, inadmissible.[5] The inadmissibility
was likely a Stanton directive. To go against it would be political suicide,
and Lew hoped for enhanced post-war political influence. As a result,
in many ways, this put Lew Wallace in a darker passage than anything
before or after. He appears to have compromised and protected two men
(Stanton and Grant) who never intended to reciprocate.

There was plenty of evidence to exculpate Wirz from a guilty verdict
and many questions concerning the prosecution's lack of fairness and

---

4. National Park Service, "Myth: Grant Stopped the Prisoner Exchange," accessed January 1, 2024, https://www.nps.
gov/ande/learn/historyculture/grant-and-the-prisoner-exchange.htm.

5. Chipman, *The Tragedy of Andersonville*, 427.

innate prejudice. However, the most bizarre part of the process was saved for last. In the closing, Colonel N.P. Chipman gave the defense and prosecution closing arguments while Wirz's attorneys were forced to look on silently. Wirz was convicted on all counts and sentenced to hang, with at least two of the counts purporting to have occurred while Wirz was clearly on sick leave and nowhere near the prison.[6]

On November 10, 1865, Henry H. Wirz was hung by the neck in the same location as the four Lincoln conspirators. Unfortunately, the hangman did not do his job properly, and Wirz's neck did not break when he fell through the trap door. He slowly and hideously strangled to death in front of a crowd of over 200 people and 120 guards.[7] His family requested his body, but they were denied. So, instead, he was buried alongside the Lincoln conspirators on prison grounds in Washington.

---

6. LaForce, "The Trial of Major Henry Wirz, A National Disgrace," 9-10.
7. University of Missouri-K.C. School of Law. "The Execution of Captain Henry Wirz," accessed January 17, 2024, http://law2.umkc.edu/Faculty/projects/FTrials/Wirz/executin.htm.

Aftermath

After Wirz's execution, his lawyer Louis Shade wrote an unprecedented and extraordinary "Open Letter to the American Public." It was published in many major newspapers around the country. He details and deftly explains how his client, Henry Wirz, was unfairly convicted. It remains one of the most damning pieces of literature ever written concerning an American injustice. He declares the military commission to have been presided over by a "despotic general."[1] Since N. P. Chipman, the judge adjutant, was a colonel, one can only assume Shade was referring to Major General Lew Wallace, the commission's president.

Public criticism grew intense when other named (or unnamed) alleged conspirators were never brought to trial and subjected to what Henry Wirz was forced to endure. Stanton was hell-bent on implicating Jefferson Davis, but neither Wirz nor anyone else would do so. Maybe that was the only justice ever served.

After the Wirz trial, Lew produced a painting he titled "Over the Dead Line." Framed inside the stockade, it was a rendition depicting the dead line fence with men being shot who crossed it. It had a formal showing at a Boston studio and received mainly positive reviews. It was considered technically well painted, too realistic for some tastes, but a credible work. Lew's likely intent was to bolster justification for another highly controversial trial and execution. A realistic depiction on canvas,

---

1. James Madison Page, *The True Story of Andersonville Prison*, (Forgotten Books, 2015 [Originally published by The Neale Publishing Company 1908]), 236.

imagining an argument that some form of justice had to be served for the atrocities committed. However, unlike the Lincoln Conspirator's painting, it did not exclude a person, as in Mary Surratt. In this case, the entire painting has gone missing and remains a mystery.

As of the publication of this book, Captain Henry H. Wirz remains the only person ever to be executed for war crimes in the United States.[2]

---

2. Tikkanen & Editors, "Andersonville," https://www.britannica.com/place/Andersonville-Georgia.

PART 5

Old and New Mexico

Cinco De Mayo

Contrary to popular belief in the United States, Cinco De Mayo is not Mexican Independence Day. In fact, in Mexico, it is known as *Día de la Batalla de Puebla* or "Battle of Puebla Day." It is a relatively minor holiday in Mexico and not widely celebrated, but it has become very popular in the United States. Many beer manufacturers claim they sell more beer on Cinco De Mayo than any other day of the year, including St. Patrick's Day, and some concede "Super Bowl Sunday" may be comparable. But this is only fitting because the United States may have benefitted more from the battle than Mexico. On May 5, 1862, a poorly trained, organized, and outfitted Mexican Army of approximately 4,000 members, led by a little-known Texas-born general, Ignacio Zaragoza, routed a French army of an estimated 8,000 French Algerian Zouaves just outside the town of Puebla, Mexico.[1]

The Mexican Army, including many indigenous people, did not stop attacking until they had forced the Zouaves back to where they began their march, Veracruz. The Zouaves were the finest troops that Napoleon III and the Second French Empire had to offer, and they had been "thoroughly thumped" by the Mexicans. Some were literally "thumped on their heads" by rock-throwing Mexican troops. Modelo runs a television ad claiming they served beer to the Mexican troops during the battle that day. Although not a significant or deciding victory, it had positive

1. Editors "Cinco de Mayo," History.com, April 29, 2022, accessed October 23, 2023, https://www.history.com/topics/holidays/cinco-de-mayo.

implications for the United States because it set the Mexico invasion plans of Napoleon III back almost a year. Eventually, 30,000 additional French troops arrived in Veracruz and marched on Mexico City, taking over the capital and ruling for three years. After the US Civil War ended, the United States secretly assisted its neighbor with weapons, ammunition, and surreptitious financial support. The Mexicans could then completely expel the French (the French version is they decided to leave).

News of the Mexican win at the Battle of Puebla against his beloved French Algerian Zouaves must have shocked Lew Wallace, giving him mixed emotions. In contrast, others in Washington and elsewhere were elated. People in California started an annual celebration, which continues across America today. Although the French claimed the right to invade Mexico to collect a long-owed debt, the United States perceived it as a pretext to invade Mexico for an eventual invasion of the United States as it was preoccupied with the Civil War. Maybe the French intended to reclaim lands lost in arguably the worst real estate deal in their history: the Louisiana Purchase. Whatever France's end game, the one-year delay allowed Abraham Lincoln to build up defenses along the Mexican border to deter any ideas the French might have of crossing into American territory. Napoleon III showed his true colors when he began to suggest his intentions in Mexico were to develop and profit from its vast riches and resources, which everyone knew the Spanish had long ago plundered.

Whatever Napolean III's long-term plans were, Cinco De Mayo was a major setback in 1862. France's defeat at Puebla helped create another opportunity for Lew Wallace. The United States government began to look differently at Mexico, first in appreciation and then as a viable deterrent to a French invasion. The last thing the United States needed was to enter another war, and it had stringent neutrality laws in effect. But they did at least start to entertain requests from President Benito Juarez for assistance, albeit under the cloak of secrecy.

While around Washington and Baltimore, Lew Wallace nurtured political relationships, particularly interested in Mexican affairs. He became friendly with Matías Romero, the Mexican ambassador to the United States. He later developed mutual respect with a charismatic Tejano, educated in the United States, who spoke fluent English. His name was

General José María Jesús Carbajal, the same General Carbajal whom Lew chased with Company H of the First Indiana Regiment near the Rio Grande during the Mexican-American War. As a young boy in Texas, Carbajal was personally mentored by "The Father of Texas," Stephen F. Austin, before becoming a dedicated Mexican citizen and soldier. As a result of his networking, Lew's name and potential value became known to the currently exiled Mexican President Benito Juarez as well. These relationships and other contacts put Lew uniquely positioned between the Mexican and United States governments, which Lew hoped to someday leverage into battlefield fame and wealth.

Old Mexico

I spend my time studying Spanish and performing duty as a spectator and listener in the Senate gallery. Of the two occupations, Spanish is the more pleasant and instructive. Once in a while I see Romero, the Mexican minister, who is very open and confidential with me. I have great interest in Mexican affairs.

—LEW WALLACE TO SUSAN WALLACE IN A LETTER
RECEIVED FROM WASHINGTON D.C. MARCH 1866[1]

Lew's involvement in Mexican affairs began after a document was created and dated November 12, 1864, signed and authorized by President Benito Juarez. The document empowered General Carbajal to purchase 40,000 rifles and other munitions abroad, enlist 10,000 foreigners into the Mexican army, and contract a foreign loan to finance these purchases and enlistments. Carbajal asked Lew for assistance in soliciting the Union's help, to which Lew agreed, and Carbajal made a trip to Washington under the assumed name of "Mr. Joseph Smith." A concerning issue with the French helped sell the idea of assisting the Mexicans. There was strong covert intelligence that the Confederacy was negotiating with the French Imperialists in Mexico to combine forces against the Union.[2] With

1. Wallace, *An Autobiography, Vol. 2*, 859.
2. Foreign Service Institute United States Department of State, Office of the Historian, "French Intervention in Mexico and the American Civil War, 1862–1867," accessed December 30, 2023, https://history.state.gov/milestones/1861-1865/french-intervention,

the deteriorating condition of the South, Grant, Stanton, and Lincoln worried such a merger could happen. Moreover, the Confederacy had leaked an additional sadistic plan of enlisting the Comanche Indians to raid and wreak havoc upon their common enemy family settlements.

Due to Mexico's pleas and the Union's continuing worries over a French/Confederate alliance, Lew was ordered to proceed to Brazos De Santiago. He was to seek out General Carbajal, who had already returned to his command in Mexico, and determine Mexico's response should the French and the Confederate armies attempt to combine. Upon arriving at the Brazos, which must have brought back disturbing memories, Lew found the Confederates camped on the east (left) side of the bank of the Rio Grande. On the west (right) side of the river, the French were camped up and down for some distance. They were poised to cross the river and quickly join the Confederates.

Lew located General Carbajal, and Carbajal committed to intervening and disrupting any attempt of the two armies to combine and enter American territory. Unfortunately, Lew's trip was cut short due to receiving word of Lincoln's assassination, and he received orders to return to Washington immediately. Shortly thereafter, the Confederacy surrendered, and Confederate General E. Kirby Smith was powerless to stop his troops from disbanding. After which, the Confederate's plans, including the unsavory Comanche alliance, were scuttled.

Monterey

*My first view of this place was through the eyes not yet twenty-one
years old. You know how enthusiastic I have always been when
speaking about the beauty of its situation. Over and over again
have I said, if this region should ever become the property of our
government, I should live in Monterey.*

—Lew Wallace to Susan Wallace in a letter
from Mexico, September 1866.[1]

On or about April 26, 1865, a letter was tendered to Major General
Lew Wallace U.S.V. by the Mexican Ambassador to the United States,
Matias Romero, tacitly approved by Secretary of State William Seward,
with threats of criminal prosecutions if Lew or Mexico should violate US
neutrality laws. Lew claimed the letter offered him a major general's commission in the Mexican service, which included substantial remuneration
and the command of a corps of American volunteers.[2] Lew stated the
offer "would secure my family beyond the chances of want, or, provision
in the event of my death."[3] Romero's letter stipulated that Lew could not
resign his commission in the United States Army until the war's progress
permitted him to do so "honorably." This provision was likely added

1. Wallace, *An Autobiography*, Vol. 2, 877.
2. Editors, *Civil War Talk*, May 11, 2017, "Major General Lew Wallace (USA)," accessed December 30, 2023, https://civilwartalk.com/threads/major-general-lew-wallace-usa.134443/.
3. Wallace, *An Autobiography*, Vol. 2, 869.

because Romero understood Seward's "neutrality caution." Lew could not be a member of the Mexican and United States armies simultaneously. For now, Mexico would have to wait for Lew's assistance because Lew was named to serve on the Lincoln Conspirator's Tribunal and then the Andersonville Conspirator's Tribunal. These tribunals dominated Lew's time for six months, until November 1865.

Lew claimed the offer from Mexico came through a letter from Romero, yet he also claimed Carbajal outlined the propositions. Nevertheless, the proposal, as Lew understood it, was never respected. A Mexican major general's commission did not materialize, the troops he recruited never deployed, and he was not paid the offered remuneration. Lew financed the fundraising and troop recruitment out of his pocket, and it took twenty years before he received any compensation. Regardless, sometime in early 1866, Lew began trying to secure financing for Mexico to buy arms and ammunition to support Mexico's efforts. He utilized one of his Baltimore staff, General Sturm, to print up bonds, and between Lew and Sturm, they raised funds in New York, selling them to investors.

General Grant had acquiesced to the fundraising, but Lew fully understood Grant would deny it should any connection become public. Sturm and Lew ran into numerous time-consuming roadblocks, too numerous and complicated to enumerate here, but eventually, they were able to secure enough funding to make purchases. Steamers were chartered to transport and deliver the contraband hidden below deck. One of the steamers was a total loss at sea. But enough arms and ammunition were provided to the Mexicans between Veracruz and Mexico City to be helpful to the cause.

After the arms deliveries were complete, Lew traveled from Matamoros to Monterey down the same road the First Indiana Regiment had marched over 200 miles eighteen years prior and over 200 miles back after Zachary Taylor turned them around six miles short of their destination. In 1848, it took a little over ten days to march to Monterey from Matamoros, and in 1866, the trip took just three in a fine, double-team carriage. Fortunately, Carbajal had previously secured Monterey and controlled most of the state of Chihuahua. Lew stayed in the area for about five months, pressing his claims to Carbajal and the Mexican government, to no avail. He only accomplished getting Carbajal to release him from providing US volunteers. Nevertheless, that was unnecessary because, from Lew's perspective, Carbajal and the Mexican government had already breached their promises. For Lew, getting that concession was likely more about maintaining his integrity after an unpleasant experience.

Except for remaining on the hook to the holders of the Mexican bonds he had sold, Lew concluded his dealings with the Mexican government in a letter to Ambassador Romero. Because of the need to hide American participation in the delivery of arms and ammunition, nearly all the activities Lew and Sturm performed were kept under the cloak of secrecy. Consequently, Lew and Sturm never received official credit for the things they had accomplished and their part in the elimination of the French from Mexico. It was another humiliating, and this time personally expensive, exploitation of Lew's honor and integrity. However, it was also, yet again, an example of his sometimes blind and naïve ambitions. To add insult to injury, eventually, the bond sales became public, and Lew was unjustifiably accused of profiting from the sales. Given his financial condition after the bond sales and the weapons deliveries, it was easy to refute those allegations. But it endured as another controversy Lew would spend the rest of his life grappling over.

The Fair God

The young author, unabashed by the somewhat austere dignity of the old president, asked permission to read to him what he had finished. Dr. White listened politely, took off his spectacles, and then gravely advised Mr. Wallace to abandon the field of authorship. He had been long in the grave when the Fair God appeared, or he might have had an opportunity to learn how little the wisest of men can forsee the fate of any book.

—Susan Wallace[1]

Lew resigned and left the US Army on November 30, 1865, and began his endeavors assisting Mexico and later trying to collect what was owed. Although he believed the Mexican government had promised him $100,000 for his services, Lew returned to the United States in 1867 empty handed and deeply in debt. He settled back into his pre-war life in Crawfordsville, practicing law while working earnestly to finish *The Fair God*. The novel he had begun to write and often set aside nineteen years before. It would be another six years before it was published, a twenty-five-year stretch from beginning to end. But Lew had an incredible focus and adherence to research and writing, which could last for more than a decade on one book.

---

1. Ibid., 894 : (Dr. Charles White was the second president of Wabash College, a lineal descendant of Peregrine White of the Mayflower, and a man of eminent scholarship. Sales of *The Fair God* from 1873 to 1905 were reported to be 145,750 copies. In those times, it was not an overwhelming success but a respectable result).

In 1870, Lew ran for Congress but was defeated. He was continually attacked during the campaign by the Democratic press for speculating on Mexican bonds. There was no proof that Lew owned Mexican bonds or profited from their sales, and he vehemently denied the reporting. But he was prohibited from explaining the details because it involved national secrecy. The damage had been done. In late 1873, once sales of *The Fair God* appeared to progress well, Lew began writing *Ben Hur*.

But like *The Fair God*, Lew's work on his new novel would be constantly interrupted over the next few years by requests to speak and appear and execute various legal tasks or political favors. Despite all the controversies in his past, Lew remained high on the list of many influential people when they required someone of high integrity and leadership ability to assist in difficult matters. In late 1876, a request came from the chairman of the state Republican committee for Lew to travel to New Orleans to be present when Louisiana counted their ballots for the 1876 presidential election. The Southern states sought an end to "reconstruction" laws and policies, which were still enforced since the Civil War's end. In addition, there were reports of voter fraud throughout the South as the Southern states sought to regain their pre-war status of independence. After a successful result in Louisiana, Lew was invited by Governor Neyes of Ohio to go to Tallahassee and witness the counting in Florida. After finishing his work in Tallahassee, Lew returned to Crawfordsville.

When Lew reached home, a telegram had already been delivered asking him to return to Tallahassee as an attorney to represent the Republican Party, specifically the apparent president-elect, Rutherford B. Hayes. A dispute was filed by Democrats contesting the results of Florida's presidential vote. Critical electoral votes were at stake to certify Hayes. Lew and the Republican team, including Governor Neyes, would successfully get the results certified by the state board. Hayes would win the presidency by a single electoral vote, and the election would mark the end of Reconstruction.[2] But before that occurred, Lew would face an unprecedented situation that he described to a reporter from the *Indianapolis Journal* upon his return:

---

2. Sheila Blackford, "Disputed Election of 1876," University of Virginia – Miller Center (2023), accessed December 30, 2023, https://millercenter.org/the-presidency/educational-resources/disputed-election-1876.

It was a matter which did not come within the scope of the common law but had to be referred to a local statute which the State of Florida enacted in 1872. This act created a board of canvassers composed of the secretary of state, the comptroller, and attorney-general, to count the vote of the several counties for presidential electors, governor, and lieutenant-governor, other state officials being appointed by the governor. If it could be shown that there had been no fraud, irregularity, or intimidation in the election, the board were required to certify to the governor the persons elected.[3]

Presidential election and vote counting legal controversies in Florida are something that's been seen in near-modern times as well (e.g., Bush v. Gore, 531 U.S. 98, (2000)).

3. Wallace, *An Autobiography, Vol. 2*, 903.

New Mexico

The United States ought to declare war on Mexico and make it take back New Mexico.

—General William T. Sherman to Territorial
Governor Lew Wallace, 1878[1]

Upon completing his duties for President Hayes and the Republican Party in Tallahassee, Lew returned to Crawfordsville. He again turned his attention to the practice of law and his latest novel, now identified as *Ben Hur*. Finally, in early 1878, he permanently retired from his legal practice, a profession he had always found distasteful. It had paid the bills for many years but, in his opinion, had never been an honorable pursuit. Lew had soured on the military and felt the "West Point Fraternity" subverted his military career and the careers of many other competent and outstanding volunteer officers.

After losing his run for Congress due mainly to blatantly false attacks on his integrity, his desire for political office appeared to wane. Most likely in appreciation for his efforts in Florida, in a letter dated August 6, 1878, Lew was offered the position of minister resident and consul general to Bolivia, with an annual salary of $5,000. This was a considerable and lucrative sum, about ten times the annual family income then and equivalent to about $500,000 today. It was money that he and his family

---

1. Thomas E. Chávez, An *Illustrated History of New Mexico*, (University of New Mexico Press – Albuquerque, 1992), 121.

badly needed. However, he politely and respectfully declined the offer in a letter to President Hayes, pointing out that the salary was not worth two years of his life and moving his family so far. It looked as though Lew had decided to stick to writing and painting.

On the contrary, two weeks later, Lew accepted an offer to become governor of the Territory of New Mexico. Upon his arrival in Santa Fé, he took residence at the Governor's Palace. It was officially a palace, but nowhere near the palaces of Europe or the Far East. Nevertheless, he wrote a letter to Susan about the structure that describes more its history than any beauty or comforts:

> *The archives of the leaky old Palacio del Gobernador hold treasures well worth the seeking of student and antiquary. The building itself has a history full of pathos and stirring incident, as the ancient fort of St. Augustine, and is older than the venerable pile. It had been the palace of the Pueblos immemorially before the holy name, Santa Fé, was given in baptism of blood by the Spanish conquerors; palace of the Mexicans after they broke away from the crown; and palace ever since its occupation by "El Gringo." In the stormy scenes of the seventeenth century it withstood several sieges; and was repeatedly lost and won, as the white man or red man held the victory.*[2]

Construction of the Governor's Palace in Santa Fe, New Mexico, began in 1609-1610 by the second official governor of the Spanish colony, Pedro de Paralta. Construction took many years. However, the building was in use by 1620, when Friar Alonzo de Benavides arrived to inspect it. The modest single-story, pueblo-style edifice was built to face Mexico City. The structure remains one of the oldest public buildings in the United States of European origin.[3] Now a museum, the interior and exterior are diligently maintained and no longer "leaky." It is upgraded with hardwood floors for comfort and safety. However, a plexiglass viewing area exists so visitors can see the original adobe brick floors and root

---

2. Wallace, *An Autobiography, Vol. 2*, 913.

3. Emily Abbink, *New Mexico's Palace of the Governors, History of an American Treasure*, (Museum of New Mexico Press 2007), 9.

cellars used for storing food, weapons, and ammunition. In one room, there is a corner adobe fireplace. On the mantle is displayed a photograph of Governor Lew Wallace. The room is named the "Ben Hur Room."[4]

It is difficult to imagine how Susan might have perceived Lew's description. She would not join him for another year, and based on his letter above, she might have had mixed emotions considering the fine home in Crawfordsville she was leaving. No one knew her husband better than she, and Lew was a master at making a silk purse out of a sow's ear with written words. But Lew found inspiration in "the leaky old Palacio" and wrote the remaining portions of one of the most successful novels ever written.

---

4. Palace visited by the author, Michael E. Fox, in October 2023.

Lawless

Kindness makes no impression upon them. They are what they were when the Spaniard found them—cunning, blood-thirsty, untamable.

—GOVERNOR LEW WALLACE TO THE TERRITORIAL LEGISLATURE OF NEW MEXICO, JANUARY 5, 1880[1]

It is not clear what Lew expected in New Mexico when he accepted the territorial governorship. Maybe the title and position convinced him, or perhaps he saw a significant challenge that could lead to recognition and fame. We know that bordering Mexico, with rich Spanish history, New Mexico was likely attractive to Lew. However, he may not have fully grasped the level of problems he was inheriting. When Lew arrived, there were two major wars in progress: one, an Indian uprising, and the other, a cattle baron war. The Indian war was led by Victorio, the chief of the Chihenne band, also known as the "Warm Springs" or "Ojo Caliente" people, one of four bands of the Chiricahua Apache tribe in the Southwestern United States. The other Apache bands, one headed by Geronimo, ranged to the west in southeastern Arizona. Victorio and his band had left the reservation and returned to Warm Springs, the ancient spiritual home of the Chihenne. The US government wanted them back on the reservation, and Victorio was not going back without a fight.

1. Wallace, *An Autobiography*, Vol. 2, 916.

Then, there was also the infamous Lincoln County War, which was still raging. The war centered around the town of Lincoln, located in southeastern New Mexico, just west of Roswell. Lincoln was the county seat of Lincoln County, covering geography comparable to all the New England states and a portion of upstate New York combined. The irony of the county's name was not lost on Lew when this became the center of significant controversy for him. Although the first battle was fought in a court of law, it eventually defied any semblance of law and order.

The murder of an English immigrant rancher, John Tunstall, ignited the out-of-court conflict. A posse of deputies from Lincoln, led by William Morton under instructions from Sheriff William Brady, rode onto Tunstall's range to demand horses. Tunstall's cattle guards saw the posse coming and tried to warn Tunstall to run. Instead, Tunstall rode to meet them. His guards heard three gunshots beyond some bushes and knew Tunstall had been gunned down. They also knew he was unarmed. With Tunstall's murder and a subsequent inquest concluding he had been shot in the back of the head, a long and bloody range war began in earnest.

/

Victorio

Lew thought Chihenne Chief Victorio was seventy-five years old when he arrived in New Mexico. However, like most so-called facts in that part of the country during that period, it was likely an exaggeration. Historians estimate Victorio's birth to be sometime in the 1820s, which would put his age in 1878 around fifty to fifty-eight. Still, Victorio maintained a strong and fearsome persona at that age. Short and muscular, he projected a sincere and soft-spoken demeanor. He had an agreeable way about him. But experienced Indian fighters perceived a calculating and ruthless warrior. Everyone agreed he was brave and wise—a master of deception and strategy, and when attacked or cornered, fearless and ruthless.

Most famous figures in those days were exaggerated to unrealistic levels. It doesn't seem to be the case with Victorio. A veteran US Army officer who chased and fought him once described Victorio as "the greatest Indian general who had ever appeared on the American continent."[1] That is an impressive compliment, putting him above all the most famous Indian chiefs before him and active at the time. However, it also acknowledged that he was the army's worst nightmare.

To make matters worse, the Chihenne had returned to their native Warm Springs and knew the location of every mountain, canyon, trail, meadow, cave, and cliff, not to mention the essential water sources. The US Army used "Apache scouts" to aid them, but they were usually from other bands and unfamiliar with the Warm Springs region. They were

---

1. Robert M. Utley, "Victorio's War," Historyet September June 2, 2008, accessed October 9, 2023, https://www.historynet.com/victorios-war/.

very valuable, however, because they could read sign, track, scout, and understand common Apache language and habits, but where the next best place to be ambushed or get water was often a search and locate exercise. Contrary to how they have sometimes been portrayed in movies, they were generally loyal and reliable. Apache scouts took an oath and gave their word. These were taken and given seriously. The word Apache came from old Spanish, meaning fundamentally "enemy," but the Apache called themselves the *Nde* or *Ndee,* meaning "the people."

The Warm Springs area was roughly between the Black Range of the Mimbres Mountains to the south and the San Mateo Mountains to the north. This area is set in the southwestern area of New Mexico in what is now mainly the Gila National Wilderness area. When hiking or traveling on horseback, changing several altitude levels in a single day is not uncommon. You can start in the early morning comfortably in shirt sleeves, and by mid-morning, you're wearing a rain slicker riding in the rain and sleet. By the afternoon, you've put on a heavy coat, covered by a slicker, to stay warm and dry from an afternoon snowstorm, maybe even blizzard conditions. Your horse must have strong lungs, tough hooves, and be well-shod because you'll likely ride through sharp lava fields created by ancient volcanos. It's not a region for weak people or horses.[2]

Luckily for the army, they had strong men, but many eastern horse breeds weren't up to the task. Eventually, the army switched to regional breeds to improve the reliability and stamina of their mounts. Sometimes, they used mules as pack mounts and rode them, as the mules had more strength and stamina and could go longer between feeding and watering. The troopers were primarily African Americans from the Ninth Cavalry. The Ninth was garrisoned in New Mexico, and the Tenth in West Texas. Most members had joined the army to escape racism and discrimination after the Civil War. African-American regiments usually had the highest reenlistment and lowest desertion rates. Since the Civil War, these regiments were stationed in the frontier's harshest and most demanding sectors.

Unfortunately for Victorio, his band was up against the bravest, toughest, and most seasoned troopers the US government had to offer.

---

2. Based on personal experience by the author, Michael E. Fox.

The Apache called the Ninth and Tenth Cavalry "Buffalo Soldiers" and later the Twenty-Fourth and Twenty-Fifth Cavalry in Texas. The Apache feared and respected them and avoided head-to-head combat if possible. African American soldiers would be awarded fourteen Congressional Medals of Honor for their bravery in the Southwest Indian Wars.[3]

---

3. National Park Service, "The Archeology of Buffalo soldiers and Apaches in the Southwest," accessed January 13, 2024, https://www.nps.gov/articles/archeology-of-buffalo-soldiers-and-apaches-in-the-southwest.htm.

Troop Request

The necessity is very great. The Comanches are in the Guadalupe Mountains southeast. The Mezcaleros on the Stanton reservation are about to break Guadalupe. Victorio's bands are already loose in Grant County. Life and property are in imminent peril.

—GOVERNOR WALLACE'S TELEGRAM TO
SECRETARY OF THE INTERIOR CARL SCHURZ
JANUARY 16, 1880[1]

In Lew's opinion, the situation was becoming desperate. He had gotten a commitment from the territorial legislature to support the recruitment of a one-thousand-man militia to help subdue the uprising. In addition, Victorio had successfully recruited other tribes to join the Chihenne cause. The dreaded Comanches and the fearsome Mezcaleros were some of their recruits. On January 16, Lew sent a letter/telegram to the secretary of the interior, Carl Schurz, asking for additional troops to be sent to the territory and to help finance the militia. On January 18, Lew received a response from Alex Ramsey, secretary of war, but signed by Schurs. The telegram said, among other things, "If the territory of New Mexico calls a thousand men for defence of her scattered settlements, the governor should be notified that the territory must pay and provide for them. It is stated that the necessity for troops has not been reported by General

1. Wallace, *An Autobiography, Vol. 2*, 917.

Hatch, who is on the spot, and that the dangers reported by Governor Lew Wallace are greatly exaggerated."[2]

Lew must have been incensed and livid. His response to Secretary Schurs was terse and sarcastic.

Hon. C. Schurs, Washington:

Answering yours of the 17th instant, I have nothing to say about remarks personal to myself therein, except that all my assertions in telegram of 16th instant rest upon letters from reliable citizens and information from General Hatch, with whom I conferred just previous to telegraphing. Unless you otherwise direct, I will to-morrow submit the answer of the secretary of war declining to send more regulars to New Mexico, and state that it is the ultimatum of the general government on that point, and that I will hasten preparations to execute the law just passed giving me men and money for defense against the Indians. As to the Comanches being more than a thousand miles from the Guadalupe Mountains of south New Mexico, people in Alabama will be astonished to hear that they have an addition to their population.

—LEW WALLACE, GOVERNOR OF NEW MEXICO [3]

Lew's response, although probably justified, was likely not well received. Three days later, he got an answer from Schurz ordering him not to recruit a militia on the premise that there was no "extreme necessity to do so."[4] Lew may have unintentionally made matters worse in his anger and no doubt tried to get the public to apply pressure on Washington. It was not long before Schur's response became known to Victorio, resulting in more bold and brutal attacks. True to his nature, despite Schur's directive, Lew organized a militia and named them "The Rifles" (after his Indianapolis militia). Lew's militia was only intended to protect lives and property. It was up to the Ninth and Tenth Cavalry to subdue Victorio and his force of more than 300.

2. Ibid., 917.
3. Ibid., 917–18.
4. Ibid., 918.

When it sometimes seemed relatively safe to travel, Lew would ride to raiding sites, express condolences, and offer support. Once, he ventured not far from Santa Fé in a coach guarded by men with Winchester rifles to visit a church, which had reported an attack resulting in multiple deaths. As they approached the community, a raiding party gathered along the surrounding ridges. The guards lifted their rifles above their heads, and the raiding party stayed out of range. Upon entering the church, Lew found sixteen corpses lying in a row in front of an altar. Multiple bashings against a wagon wheel severely mutilated one small boy's head. The townspeople were surprised that the governor had made it to the church alive.

The atrocities were many and sometimes very personal for Lew. For example, a good friend, Judge McComas, while traveling with his family, was ambushed and murdered by a raiding party. The family's bodies were later found lying beside the road, badly mutilated.[5] Washington's insensitivity to the plight of the New Mexican people during this brutal uprising has never been forgotten. It finally took a combination of US and Mexican soldiers and volunteers in Chihuahua, in an effort of extreme bravery and skill, to end the madness.

The US Calvary, after nine more months of relentless pursuit, chased Victorio across the border into Mexico. Victorio's people were desperate for water, meat, and rest by this time. Unbeknownst to the US Cavalry or Mexican authorities, the band was also running short of ammunition. In mid-October 1880, the band was spotted by a Mexican lake near some rocky peaks named *Tres Castillos* (Three Castles), located in the Mexican state of Chihuahua, south of El Paso. They were camped, roasting some stolen cattle. With a force of approximately 350, a Mexican colonel, Joaquin Terrazas, attacked Victorio's encampment and drove the band to the south side of the mountain peaks. Men, women, and children ran on foot for their lives. With the steep slopes directly behind them, they moved large rocks together to create a fortification against a Mexican attack.

Colonel Terrazas was not deterred. His force attacked the rocks, caves, and slopes and systematically killed or captured most of Victorio's braves.

5. Ibid., 919.

Some of the Mezcaleros were away then, and other Braves escaped. No one knows how Victorio died, but he was found dead and identified. Legend has it he took his own life with a knife rather than be captured because his band had run out of ammunition; only one unspent bullet was found next to all the Braves who were killed. The Mexicans lost just three men.[6] Before Victorio's demise and his coalition were crushed, an estimated 400 people perished in and around New Mexico. The territory's citizens endured considerable destruction and loss, besides the senseless murders and mutilations.

6. Utley, "Victorio's War," https://www.historynet.com/victorios-war/.

Lincoln County

When I reached Santa Fé, I found that law was practically a nullity, and had no way of asserting itself. The insurrection seemed to be confined to one county, which, strangely enough, was called Lincoln [. . .]. I could not have possibly have stopped that trouble by civil means, and, accordingly, I was forced to result to arms [. . .]. I forwarded these combined statements to President Hayes, and asked him to proclaim an insurrection in New Mexico, which he did [. . .]. I finally had four companies of cavalry for two months, and at the end of that time the desperados were driven out of the country, the armed factions were broken up, and the best grazing section of country in the United States was open to immigrants.

—LEW WALLACE[1]

The above excerpts from Lew's writings about his time in New Mexico sound good, and most likely, per Lew's memories, he believed them true, but they are only partially accurate. Nevertheless, being very close to declaring martial law, Lew instead used some force of military presence, combined with an astute move of amnesty, to set the stage for eventual peace. Although many historians believe Lew's proclamation of amnesty

1. Wallace, *An Autobiography, Vol. 2*, 914–915.

for all involved in the Lincoln County War on November 13, 1878, officially marked the end of the conflict, it is more involved than that.

Many participants, like Billy Bonney (a.k.a. Billy the Kid), had already been indicted for the murder of Buckshot Roberts and Sheriff William Brady, so Lew's amnesty did not include those killings. Many indictments hung around for years, and sporadic acts of vengeance relating to the War continued into 1884. One early example is Alexander McSween's widow hiring an attorney named Huston Chapman to seek recompense against James Dolan for killing her husband. Chapman was murdered on February 18, 1879, and James Dolan was accused. Dolan later used his influential friends to get the charges dropped. In the meantime, he purchased property previously owned by John Tunstall, to whose murder he was also linked.

The Lincoln County War started between rival cattle barons. In the early 1870s, two men named Lawrence Murphy and James Dolan owned the only mercantile store and commercial bank in Lincoln County. They had a virtual monopoly in the county regarding selling supplies and financing real estate and cattle deals. It was very lucrative because Lincoln was the largest county in the United States. They also bought up land and ran a large cattle operation. Their hands were in every part of the county's commerce. They became locally known as the "House."

In 1877, a young and wealthy immigrant Englishman named John Tunstall set his sights on starting a sheep operation in New Mexico but quickly changed his mind to cattle. He started buying land to establish an operation but realized Murphy and Dolan were working to undermine his efforts. Tunstall sought and found two independent men who disliked the House: a lawyer named Alexander McSween and a wealthy rancher, John Chisum, who ran more than 100,000 head of cattle. Tunstall convinced them to become partners, and they set up a rival business to the House, which they named H.H. Tunstall & Company. Serious conflicts and confrontations resulted.

Tunstall was not aggressive or violent, but Murphy and Dolan were, and they tried to goad Tunstall into a deadly confrontation, which he refused to engage. Murphy and Dolan's frustrations grew, and Tunstall realized he needed to hire men to protect his assets on the range and in the store, so he started hiring men he called "cattle guards." Of course, a cattle guard infers more than just a cowpuncher, and the men Tunstall hired came with certain reputations and skill sets necessary to be guards. One of the people he hired was going by the name of Billy Bonney. Thought to be about seventeen in 1877, Tunstall nonetheless sensed a high level of self-confidence in the young man and was surprised by his good manners, intelligence, and ability to read and write. Not to mention that he was already an excellent horseman and crack shot with a revolver and Winchester rifle.

Many have tried to establish a strong relationship between Tunstall and Bonney, but Tunstall was likely too busy and English elevated to fraternize with his guards. However, he gave Billy a good horse, saddle, and two new pistols when he hired on. That was likely the only kind and generous gesture Billy had experienced in his life, and it's unlikely Tunstall understood he had created passionate loyalty from a very dangerous and lethal young killer.

Clandestine Meeting

Come to the house of old Squire Wilson at nine (9) o'clock next Monday night alone [. . .]. I have authority to exempt you from prosecution if you will testify to what you say you know. The object of the meeting at Squire Wilson's is to arrange the matter in a way to make your life safe. To do that the utmost secrecy is to be used. So come alone. Don't tell anybody—not a living soul—You are coming or the object. If you could trust Jesse Evans, you can trust me.

—GOVERNOR LEW WALLACE'S NOTE TO BILLY THE KID
MARCH 15, 1879 [1]

We will probably never know where Billy Bonney or "Billy the Kid" was born and who his biological father was. Constant research over 140 years has continued to lead historians in circles. However, that is a lot of the fun and excitement of studying Billy the Kid and what perpetuates the obsession. Where he was born, and certain people thought he was, is more important than the actual place. After all, most common beliefs concerning Billy are just that, beliefs not based on indisputable evidence.

Billy the Kid and Lew Wallace had one documented thirty-minute clandestine meeting in Lincoln, New Mexico. The Kid's friends would say that when he heard Lew Wallace was arriving to be the territorial

1. Frederick Nolan, *The West of Billy the Kid*, (University of Oklahoma Press, Norman 1998), 195.

governor of New Mexico, Billy commented that he and the new governor might get along because they were both from Indiana.[2] The Kid's supposed comment is hearsay at best, but we know Billy had a reputation for being a charming, poker-playing con man. There is every reason to believe he would try and charm Lew by repeating his mother's verbal claims to people in Silver City, New Mexico, that his birthplace was Anderson, Indiana.[3] There is no indisputable evidence to prove this, as all birth records from Anderson were destroyed in a courthouse fire in 1880.

Lew and General Hatch of the Ninth Cavalry arrived together in Lincoln on March 1, 1879. Lew was moved to action by the murder of the widow of McSween's lawyer, Huston Chapman. Lew wrote about meeting with the Kid in Lincoln in his autobiography and acknowledged promising him amnesty in exchange for his testimony against men involved with the House and others. The meeting occurred on March 17, after the Kid wrote a letter to Lew dated March 13, offering his cooperation. Having had a tough time getting locals to come forward, Lew was elated and wrote the note quoted above to the Kid to set up the meeting. Both parties were anxious to please, and very likely, personal details and pleasantries were exchanged.

After the meeting, Lew arranged a mock arrest of Billy on March 21 to not raise suspicion. On April 14, Billy testified to a grand jury as he promised. The grand jury eventually brought forward 200 indictments. After Billy testified, he was taken back into custody. The Kid vehemently protested his detainment but to no avail. The local prosecutor, William Rynerson, not a friend to territory law enforcement, explained to Billy that Governor Wallace had no authority to offer amnesty for the Kid's alleged murders of Buckshot Roberts and Sheriff William Brady. Therefore, the Kid would remain in custody and await trial.

2. Indy., "Billy the Kid was a famous Old West outlaw, But Indiana ties shaped his roots and fate," accessed January 17, 2024, https://www.indystar.com/story/entertainment/arts/2023/11/01/billy-the-kid-old-west-outlaw-indianapolis-anderson-indiana-ties/70662161007/.

3. Stephen T. Jackson, "In History: Was Billy the Kid from Anderson?" *Herald Bulletin*, Anderson, Indiana, June 19, 2014, accessed October 23, 2023, https://www.heraldbulletin.com/archives/in-history-was-billy-the-kid-from-anderson/article_b6579798-ac8e-553b-a204-37a35ba9fe80.html.

The Kid Escapes

While awaiting trial, Billy wrote letters asking Lew to fulfill his promise and intervene. Lew must have concluded he had overstepped his authority or decided intervening was a bad idea for some reason. Either way, he never responded to Billy's letters and did nothing. Billy gave up hope of a pardon, and on June 17, with the help of his friend Tom O'Folliard, walked out of jail, saddled up a horse, and rode for Fort Sumner. Incidents and stories attributed to the Kid continued through November 1880, while Billy spread word of his intent to kill Lew Wallace. In early December 1880, Lew distributed a wanted poster with a $500 reward for the Kid's capture to all county sheriffs in New Mexico.

In the early hours of December 10, 1880, a fire was discovered in the Madison County Clerk's Office in Anderson, Indiana, estimated to have started between three and five in the morning. The town had no organized fire department, and while volunteers tried to extinguish the flames, the effort was in vain. The county's official records were lost, including all birth records, and the fire's source remains a mystery. Some newspapers around the state printed a story that an itinerant Irishman from Kokomo named Frank Moreland had confessed to setting the fire while drunk. *The Anderson Newspaper* wrote that a vagrant (who was never named) was arrested but released for lack of evidence. Moreland's name does not appear in the history of any city records, and no history ever written about the incident attempts to explain the origins of the fire.[1] If Billy the Kid's birth record was in the courthouse, it was destroyed.

1. Beth Oliace, "Blaze burns away county records," (*The Herald Bulletin*, Anderson, Indiana, December 22, 2012), accessed October 21, 2023, https://www.heraldbulletin.com/community/blaze-burns-away-county-records/article_64141797-94b6-5565-a0c9-570bf2bedff6.html.

In mid-December 1880, Sheriff Pat Garrett of Lincoln County cornered and arrested Billy the Kid near Stinking Springs, New Mexico. The Kid was tried for murder and sentenced to hang. Lew Wallace signed his death warrant. While awaiting execution in Lincoln, Billy escaped again killing two deputies in the process and went on the lam.

In a letter dated May 19, 1881, Lew received a commission from newly elected President James A. Garfield, naming him the United States resident minister to Turkey. Lew and Garfield met and fought together at Shiloh and remained friends through the years. Lew and Susan departed Santa Fé for Turkey shortly after receiving Garfield's commission.[2]

Around 12:30 A.M. on July 14, 1881, Pat Garrett gunned down Billy the Kid in Ft. Sumner, New Mexico, in a manner many have described as an execution. Garrett claimed that while sneaking up on the home of the Kid's friend, Pete Maxwell, he saw a figure moving in the dark that looked like Billy. Garrett decided to enter Pete Maxwell's bedroom to awaken and question him whether Billy was about, leaving two accompanying deputies outside by a fence. While walking around the house, Billy heard or saw the deputies by the fence. He quickly spun around, drawing his pistol and asking, "Who is it?" numerous times while backing into Pete Maxwell's bedroom. Upon entering Pete's bedroom, Billy sensed someone else besides Pete and spun around, facing the bed while asking, "Who is it?" Pete Maxwell exclaimed to Garrett, "It's him," meaning it was Billy. Garrett quickly responded by drawing his revolver and firing. Billy fell, moaned for a bit, and went silent. Pete Maxwell ran out to another room, grabbed a candle, and lit it. In the meantime, Garrett exited the bedroom and stood outside. Maxwell shined the candle through a window into his bedroom, and he could see a body lying on the floor. He and Deluvina Maxwell, a family housekeeper, entered the room and confirmed it was Billy and that he was dead. In the morning, a coroner's jury was convened, and the killing was deemed justifiable. Billy was taken to Pete Maxwell's carpenter shop, laid into a coffin, and buried on the grounds where it remains today.[3]

---

2. General Lew Wallace Study & Museum, "Diplomat," accessed January 13, 2024, https://www.ben-hur.com/meet-lew-wallace/diplomat/.

3. Nolan, *The West of Billy the Kid*, 285–89.

Sister Blandina Segale

Sister Blandina was stationed at Steubenville, Ohio, when she received a letter from the Motherhouse in Cincinnati, telling her to proceed to Trinidad for missionary work. Hastening to obey, Sister Blandina confided to her sister, Sister Justina, that she believed her happy destination to be an island off the coast of Venezuela. [1]

Any discussion of New Mexico and Lew Wallace in the 1870s and 1880s would not be complete without including Sister Blandina Segale. She is a New Mexico historical figure the Vatican is currently vetting in Rome for sainthood. She is not yet canonized, but her initial case presentation was accepted for study and consideration. It was officially logged in 2015, but the process could take several years. She is the first to be accepted for consideration in New Mexico churches' four hundred and twenty-five-year history. Sister Blandina, at twenty-two, arrived at her first missionary station on December 9, 1872. It was Trinidad, a little mining town in southwestern Colorado, not the island in the Caribbean she first thought. She traveled there alone, first by rail and then by mule coach on a long trek across the open plains. She was warned she could be stranded for weeks by snowstorms and to stay away from cowboys. The poor young lady was terrified but never wavered.

---

1. Sister Blandina Segale, *At the End of the Santa Fé Trail*, (Pathfinder's Books, 2014), 11.

Maria Rosa Segale was born on January 23, 1850, in Cicagna, Italy, a small mountain village near Genoa. Her father was an illiterate peasant, and her mother was a foundling.[2] In search of a better life, the entire family immigrated to the United States in 1854. They settled in the predominantly German immigrant city of Cincinnati. Religions consisted primarily of Catholic, Lutheran, Reformed, and Jewish, but there was a substantial population of Catholics. At sixteen, she took her vows as a Sister of Charity, taking the name of "Sister Blandina Segale," her sister also took her vows as "Sister Justina Segale." Sister Blandina taught school for several years in Ohio until she received her orders to proceed to Trinidad.

Four years before taking her vows, in September of 1862, when Maria Segale was twelve and the Civil War was in full swing, Confederate Generals E. Kirby Smith and Braxton Bragg moved their armies into Kentucky, threatening to invade Cincinnati. A young but competent major general in the Union Army soon arrived to take over its defense named Lew Wallace. In 1878, after Sister Blandina had moved to Santa Fé in 1876, following four years in Trinidad, she was pleased to learn Lew was coming to New Mexico as the new governor. However, she eerily predicted his time in New Mexico would be too short to accomplish everything needed, for the territory had become extremely dangerous and corrupt.

Sister Blandina wrote to her sister Justina: "The last governor made himself obnoxious to the native population [. . .]. His successor, Lew Wallace, is above reproach, a man of strong principles, and a student of humanity. Such characters are seldom left where they can accomplish most good. Whatever the cause, this is apparent."[3] On October 1, 1878, she again wrote Justina, "Our new Governor [. . .]. It is difficult to predict anything about him, except that he has a difficult task before him. Not the least of which will be to check the depredations being committed by Billy and his gang."[4]

---

2. A foundling is a baby who has been either abandoned or left somewhere to be discovered.
3. Segale, *At the End of the Santa Fé Trail*, 72-73.
4. Ibid., 98.

Sister and Lew

Unfortunate 'Billy the Kid!' His marauding has drawn the atten-
tion of the whole Territory and the "Kid" is as confident of safety
as though he had a battalion at his command. It has been bruited
about that he intends undoing Governor Wallace. Friends of law
and order are on the qui vive that no harm come to the author of
Ben Hur.

—Sister Blandina Segale to her sister Justina,
March, 1881[1]

After six years in the territory and now twenty-eight years old, but already twelve years a nun, Sister Blandina developed a rugged and practical core. She had witnessed lynchings and murders, Indian attacks and
mutilations, and the aftermaths of bloody retaliations by the Ninth and
Tenth Cavalry. She was under no delusion that anything would change
in the short term, and criticism of Lew was starting to circulate. Word
spread that he was more interested in writing his novel than tending to
the territory's issues. Lew admitted to locking himself into a back room
of the palace for hours and days at a time so as not to be interrupted.[2]

Sister Blandina does not mention personal meetings with Lew, but
she was well known to him by reputation, and he received notes of requests from her. It would not have been proper in those days for a nun
to visit the palace and personally seek favors, but we know Lew provided

1. Ibid., 148.
2. Wallace, *An Autobiography,* Vol. 2, 921–25.

her the authority to travel where she wished and see whom she pleased, even in jails, including Billy the Kid. It may be many years before we know whether Sister Blandina is recognized as a saint by the Catholic Church, but Lew appears to have recognized her as exceptional.[3]

At one point, the Sister did express some disfavor towards Lew. It was concerning another man's religious beliefs, not his policies and actions as governor. It was the Sister's perception Lew had developed a friendship with Robert G. Ingersoll, "The Great Agnostic," who popularized a higher criticism of the Bible, a humanistic philosophy, and scientific rationalism. He was extremely famous at the time, and although controversial, it was considered a great honor to meet him—but not for the Sister. A local and cultured man visited her at her convent and asked if she would like to meet Mr. Ingersoll, and he would be glad to bring him over.

"Not at all, Sir," was the Sister's response. She continued, "I understand our estimable Governor has received him at the Palace several times?"

"Yes, Sister, he has. May I bring Mr. Ingersoll?" was the man's response.

"No, thank you. I forfeit the honor," she replied.[4]

In a later letter to her sister Justina, Sister Blandina shared a story she had heard.

> Governor Lew Wallace and Mr. Ingersoll were on a train from Santa Fé to Las Vegas. Mr. Ingersoll, looking at the mountains of white clouds and their background of perfect blue, addressed Mr. Wallace in this form: Wallace, what is beyond those clouds? [. . .] ether? What beyond that space? And then [. . .] I don't know. Do you? Mr. Wallace made no reply. When his book, Ben Hur, came from the publisher, one copy was forwarded to Mr. Ingersoll with this statement: This is the answer to your questions to me on the train from Santa Fé to Las Vegas.[5]

So, Lew may have redeemed himself concerning his perceived friendship with Mr. Ingersoll after Sister Blandina read Ben Hur.

---

3. Segale, *At the End of the Santa Fé Trail*, 115.
4. Ibid., 98.
5. Ibid., 98-99.

PART 6

Ben Hur

When I reach the words 'The End,' how beautiful they will look to me! What a long, long work it has been, a labor of love! How many hours and days and weeks it has consumed! Frightful to think of; and yet I know no happier way of passing time, none which takes me so completely out of this world and affairs of the present, a perfect retreat from the annoyances of daily life as they are spun for me by enemies, and friends who might as well be enemies.

—LEW WALLACE[1]

---

1. Wallace, *An Autobiography, Vol. 2*, 924–25.

Commercial Appeal

Ben Hur is often touted as the most significant religious book of the nineteenth century, second only to the Bible, but God or Jesus Christ are not its main characters. Lew was cautious not to make Jesus the main character because books written that way were usually commercially unsuccessful. People preferred only one book with God or Jesus Christ as its protagonist, the Bible. Nevertheless, Jesus appears early in *Ben Hur*, in the middle, and again towards the end. Lew even refers to him primarily as "The Nazarene." He was masterful in his design and steps around it, but never directly into the character.

Nonetheless, the result is a book often quoted as the Bible, and the movies replayed every religious holiday as a biblical story. Lew began the project as a fill-in story about three wise men briefly written about in the book of Mathew. When Lew first read about these men in Centerville, Indiana, he wanted to give them names, faces, fancy clothes, camels, countries, religions, and personalities. At some point during his early efforts, he had an epiphany, and *Ben Hur* evolved into something much more. When Lew handed the manuscript to his publisher, they were skeptical but, a year later, amazed. The reason is that *Ben Hur* is not a religious novel, per se; it is a story with all the elements of what was popular to write and read in 1880, the same elements that dominate popular stories today. It's first about jealousy, greed, lies, slavery, poverty, gambling, overindulgence, disease, bigotry, death, and vengeance. By first exposing the reader to all these negative traits, Lew sets the stage to transition the reader to the positives of honesty, compassion, justice, generosity, loyalty, friendship, family, glory, love, and redemption.

Lew understood exactly what he was creating and missed no element of entertaining human interest. People still think of the book as a religious story because it includes the birth, miracles, crucifixion, and resurrection of Jesus. That's the brilliant illusion and the testament to its greatness. Lew never claimed to be religious, although he claimed personal spirituality and a belief in a higher order. What he created and what we treasure and enjoy is entirely different. It's a story of human nature, with all the good and bad traits laid bare in one brilliant work. The fact the story includes Jesus Christ and Christianity is a bonus.

Characters

> *The very beginning of the book lies in a quotation from St.
> Matthew: 'Now when Jesus was born in Bethlehem of Judea, in
> the days of Herod the king, behold, there came wise men from the
> east to Jerusalem, saying, Where is He that is born King of the
> Jews? For we have seen His star in the east and are come to wor-
> ship Him.' Far back as my memory goes of things read by or to
> me, those lines took a hold on my imagination beyond every other
> passage of Scripture. How simple they are! But analyze them, and
> behold the points of wonder! The saying that they came from the
> east is altogether unsatisfactory. How many were they? And oh,
> the star! The star!*
>
> —LEW WALLACE[1]

There's no doubt Lew considered commercial appeal as he wrote *Ben
Hur,* but many believe it's also the veiled story of his life. One of the most
significant personal setbacks he experienced was the Battle of Shiloh.
Lew spent much of his life trying to correct and rewrite the narrative and
blamed Grant and Rawlins for much of it. Most likely, the accidental
dislodging of the roof tile by Ben Hur that inadvertently drops on the

---

1. Ibid., 926 : The only reference to these men in the Bible is in Chapter 2 of the Gospel of Matthew, and they're
not called "wise men," or "kings." Instead, they were called "Magi," which may translate into "wise men." There's also no
mention of how many men there were and only mentions they were from the "east".

Roman military commander, "Valerius Gratus," introduces a character that was meant to portray Ulysses S. Grant. Grant came from near impoverishment in Illinois to a commanding military status at Shiloh and had a similar path as Gratus from Rome to Judea. Grant was desperate to attain notoriety and success for himself and his family. This was the same desire of Gratus in *Ben Hur*, but unlike Grant in real life, Lew made sure Gratus failed. Lew came to his military position via political connections, and Grant came to his position after rekindling a previously disappointing military career. Grant was a West Point graduate, and Lew was a "political soldier." Gratus was a Roman soldier with legion training, and Judah Ben Hur was not. Lew fully understood all these negative undercurrents flowing from Grant and portrayed a similar scenario for Judah Ben Hur and his treatment by Gratus.

Ben Hur's childhood friend Messala is more challenging to compare. He likely represents Indiana Governor Oliver P. Morton. Morton was four years older than Lew but attended Professor Hoshour's academy in Centerville, Indiana, before Lew's arrival. Lew always recognized his year in Centerville as the defining year of his childhood. When Lew attended the academy, Morton was serving as a hatter's apprentice in town. If he had not met Morton in Centerville, he certainly would have later through his father, David, or his brother-in-law, Henry S. Lane. Lane and Morton worked closely together in the Republican Party. Before then, Morton was a Democrat like Lew, left to join the People's Party, a short-lived left-wing populist party, before joining the Republicans. As a result, Lew and Morton openly expressed public political and philosophical differences before the Civil War, just as Judah Ben Hur and Messala did in *Ben Hur*. However, Morton called on Lew in a crisis, and Lew showed his loyalty and willingness to put differences aside and assist Morton, Indiana, and his country.

Thanks to Lew's hard work and exceptional recruiting abilities, Morton became a shining star in Washington. When Halleck and Stanton directed Morton to put Lew on the shelf after Shiloh, Lew felt betrayed, just as Messala betrayed Judah Ben Hur, sending him to the galleys after his innocent mistake. From then forward, Lew had little to say or do with Morton. Morton later suffered a series of strokes, which left him mostly paralyzed, and he died in 1877. In the fifth part of *Ben Hur*, Judah Ben Hur goads Messala into a wager greater than Messala's entire wealth. He then sets about to destroy Messala physically, socially, and financially.

Simonides may very likely be a symbol character for Henry S. Lane. Lew did not often mention Lane; however, he and Susan named their only son after him, Henry Lane Wallace. Lane was a very astute politician and businessman but projected the persona of a country bumpkin. He had a habit of constantly chewing tobacco and was missing his front teeth. Lew described Lane as a well-liked, though somewhat disheveled, officer during the Mexican-American War. This later description of Lane might have been tainted a bit by jealousy, as Lane was more politically successful than Lew and often thought the preferred son-in-law of Isaac Elston. Lane also developed an enviable friendship with Abraham Lincoln that Lew never had. Still, Lane remained loyal to Lew and constantly reminded Lincoln of Lew's accomplishments and abilities.

When Lew was gone for long periods, Lane was the reliable brother-in-law who helped look after his family and affairs. Lane may have also played the facilitator role with Isaac Elston concerning family issues. In any case, Lew could have considered Lane's place in his life as Judah Ben Hur considered Simonides—a trusted friend, but not on equal levels in some ways. Simonides' daughter became Judah Ben Hur's wife, and her name choice, Esther, Lew's birth mother's name, is interesting. Lew never gives Judah *Ben Hur*'s birth mother a name in his book. He describes Esther very similarly to how he first describes his wife, Susan. Judah Ben Hur does not find Esther strikingly beautiful, and when Lew first meets Susan, his reaction is comparable. Lew chose Susan for her fine qualities and sensibilities, and as time passed, the attraction grew as it did with Esther in *Ben Hur*.

The three wise men in *Ben Hur* are a variation of other versions told worldwide. Very little detail is mentioned about them in the Bible, and Lew's version was conjured and written before he came upon the greater purpose of his project. It uses some names, countries, and religions of previously written versions, the most similar of which exists in Spain but was first seen in Italy sometime in the sixth century. A minister from Missouri once claimed Lew stole the story from a Hebrew version, but

Lew sued the man and prevailed, and the minister was suspended for a year. In many ways, it does not fit the rest of the novel. Each man is from a different country with diverse religions. Lew weaves them into traveling partners with their distinct appearance, personality, and character.

One of the wise men is named Balthasar. Balthasar's daughter Iras is a symbol of infatuation. She shows her narcissism by asking Judah Ben Hur to call her "Egypt." She is deceitful and uses her relationship with him to seek power and wealth. Iras is either a symbol for someone in Lew's life or a personification of the treachery Lew often experienced. Related to Iras is not a character but a place, the intriguing "Grove," where Judah Ben Hur wanders, full of pagan pleasures and numerous temptations. He decides one day to remain and partake in all its offerings until he is struck with a strong sense of family and responsibility. The Grove could symbolize his many months in Monterey, Mexico, where Lew wandered and told Susan he wanted to live. It makes one wonder if he ever seriously considered it.

The chariot race in the circus is the climaxing event when Judah Ben Hur finally reveals his identity to Messala. The race symbolizes the ultimate spectacle of competition and bravado before a crowd of thousands. In literary form, at least, it fulfills Lew's dream of fame on the battlefield and allows him to exact long-awaited revenge on Messala (Morton). It also gives local recognition of Judah Ben Hur being formally trained as a Roman soldier (i.e., West Point graduate) by his adopted father in Rome, Quintas Arrius (Quintus Arrius was an actual Roman praetor in 73 BC).[2] Judah Ben Hur's competitive behavior on the track does not display a sense of fairness or Christianity when he runs over and breaks one of Messala's wheels, causing him to crash and be severely injured. Furthermore, he never shows remorse for Messala's resulting physical disabilities and financial destruction.

Judah Ben Hur does, however, show good nature by asking Simonides to only return to him the value of the House of Hur at the time he was sent to the galleys, but Simonides could retain the profits

---

2. A praetor in ancient Rome was a judicial officer with broad authority in equity cases. Lew Wallace no doubt picked the name, Quintas Arius, from ancient Rome because praetors were considered fair men trusted to make equitable decisions.

that had accumulated.[3] Simonides, in turn, bribes a Roman official so that Pontius Pilot replaces Gratus, and Gratus is no longer a threat to Judah Ben Hur and the House of Hur. When Pontius Pilot arrives, he has the prisons inspected, and through this process, Judah Ben Hur's mother and sister, who have been jailed since Judah's enslavement, are released. Unfortunately, they contracted leprosy during this period and were banished to live in a leper colony. Judah Ben Hur's mother and sister are eventually cured of leprosy by Jesus, and the family is reunited. One can only speculate that Lew was thinking of his biological mother and younger brother, who died of disease, and how his childhood might have been different had they lived.

In the book's final sections, Ben Hur witnesses the crucifixion of Jesus, which profoundly affects him. He becomes a Christian and thus discards hatred and vengeance. Additionally, he devoted himself to good works and charity, providing the funds and resources to build an underground shelter in Rome to protect Christians from executions and general persecution. Lew was certainly no stranger to executions. He was partly responsible for a few, and I'm sure he witnessed others, not to mention all the deaths he saw in the Mexican-American and Civil Wars. After a time, we can only assume it became overwhelming, and as he aged, the burdens became heavier. Some are skeptical that Lew became a dedicated Christian after writing *Ben Hur*, but if you consider *Ben Hur* not just as a story in a book but as an in-depth reflection of a man's life and soul, then the concept of a profound change seems possible.

Lew said he could remember almost precisely when the idea emerged to write *Ben Hur*. That's believable, except the idea was not likely inspired by one night on a train or by one person on that train. It was more likely a culmination of life's experiences that had marinated for years and was ready to cook.

---

3. This gesture could reflect Lew's real-life challenge of understanding his finances and failing to accumulate net assets until his son took over handling his business and financial affairs in later years.

Method

*Ponder the task! There was but one method open to me. I ex-
amined catalogues of books and maps, and sent for everything
likely to be useful. I wrote with a chart always before my eyes—a
German publication, showing the towns and villages, all sacred
places, the heights, the depressions, the passes, trails, and distances.*

—LEW WALLACE[1]

Many people think when a novel is written, it is based purely on a writer's personal experiences and observations. This is generally untrue. One
successful contemporary writer confesses to ordering 200 to 300 books
to read and research before writing what is thought to be a spontaneous
novel. Lew Wallace admitted that he spent far more time reading in various libraries, ordering and studying maps than in actual writing. This was
normal then and is typical today. After thousands of documented ideas
and multiple works, pulling an original story out of a hat is nearly impossible. A writer needs specific details and storytelling inspirations to keep
them motivated and filled with something to create and write. A novel
typically starts as a simple idea or story that the writer fills with scenarios
and information from other sources to complete the process. Many today
even use a "standard recipe" in each book. However, it should be noted

1. Wallace, *An Autobiography Vol.2*, 932.

that in Lew's time, writers with his originality and free imagination were few and far between.

There is a story when Lew visited the Holy Land many years after the publication of *Ben Hur*, a journalist asked him if it was as he remembered. Lew responded, "This is my first time seeing it." Some historians have made the error of suggesting Lew knew little about maps and topography, even going so far as suggesting his perceived error at Shiloh was due to his inexperience with maps. This seems untrue. Remember in Covington when Lew was a child, and his new teacher handed him two books, one of math and one of geography? Lew set the math book aside, devoured the geography book, and soon drew maps, including sketches of battlefield landscapes. The truth is, Lew knew precisely where he was at Shiloh. The controversy was whether he was ordered to take River Road or whether he had the choice of which route to take; he chose the Shunpike. Although most likely not funny to Lew, many have joked that the name Shunpike alone should have given him pause.

Lew was later somewhat vindicated after a reunion at Shiloh, where Lew rode, redrew, and illustrated his route. The participants generally agreed that he had made the correct decision, given the orders as thought to have been communicated to him. Interestingly, Grant's understanding of the area and terrain has since been questioned more than Lew's. After the end of the Civil War and just after Grant's memoirs were first printed, the widow of General W. H. L. Wallace sent a copy of a letter to Grant written by her husband just before the Battle of Shiloh, dated April 5, 1862. That morning, General W.H.L. Wallace and Lew had agreed, after careful study and examination in a situation of necessity to get reinforcements from the river to the battlefield, that the Shunpike was the shorter and faster route. After reading the letter, Grant changed his tone concerning Lew and Shiloh. Included in the next printing, in a special note, Grant conceded, "This (letter) modifies very materially what I have said, and what has been said by others, of the conduct of General Lew Wallace at the Battle of Shiloh."[2]

---

2. Robert & Katherine Morseberger, *Lew Wallace: Militant Romantic*, (McGraw-Hill Book Company 1980), 353.

Inspiration

It is possible to fix the hour and place of the first thought of a book precisely enough; that was a night in 1876. I had been listening to discussion which involved such elemental points as God, heaven, life hereafter, Jesus Christ, and His divinity. Trudging on in the dark, alone except as one's thoughts may be company good or bad, a sense of the importance of the theme struck me for the first time and with a force both singular and persistent.

—LEW WALLACE [1]

The night Lew refers to above is thought to be the night of a train trip from Washington to Indianapolis to attend the Third National Soldier's Reunion. On the train with him, sitting in a private compartment, was Roger G. Ingersoll. Ingersoll was a famous circuit speaker now swept under the rug of faded history. Ingersoll has been called "The Great Free Thinker," "The Great Agnostic," "The Great Atheist," and "The American Infidel," depending on what circle of influence you ask. He had been a Colonel in the Eleventh Illinois Cavalry, serving under Brigadier General Benjamin M. Prentiss at the Battle of Shiloh. Lew and Ingersoll spent years acting, saying, and even writing like they had never known each other, but it's hard to believe they hadn't at least met on a few occasions.

---

1. Wallace, *An Autobiography Vol. 2*, 929.

One of the regiments of the Eleventh Illinois Cavalry, Third Battalion, was under Lew Wallace's command at Shiloh. Ingersoll had recruited and created the Eleventh Illinois Cavalry, so they met at Shiloh or were familiar with each other at the very least.[2] As the story goes, Ingersoll recognized Lew's voice on the train and invited Lew into his private compartment to meet. The two men purportedly spent a few hours debating faith, religion, and various other subjects. It's believed this discussion was the catalyst and inspiration for Lew to progress *Ben Hur* beyond the three wise men. But, of course, it's hard to believe Ingersoll was the sole inspiration for Lew. Besides, he began researching and writing *Ben Hur* in 1873, and his supposed spontaneous meeting with Ingersoll occurred in 1876. However, Ingersoll was an incredibly gifted lawyer, speaker, and philosopher. He famously influenced many judges, juries, politicians, contemporary philosophers, and free thinkers, so it's not impossible he influenced Lew Wallace.

At the risk of sounding disrespectful, there are three other possible inspirations: money, fame, and vindication. Lew had debts, and his constant, lengthy absences from his law practice may have hurt his business. It undoubtedly became more challenging for him to find and retain clients. Lew needed another career and source of income; *The Fair God* was a modest success and provided revenue, so writing another novel must have looked like the best option. His publisher encouraged him, and he was then a known literary name. Like many others, Lew had tried the speaking circuit but had limited success, and travel was expensive and time-consuming. Unfortunately, he was not Robert Ingersoll, but he wanted the same fame and fortune. Another successful novel would hopefully provide the recognition he desired. Lew also needed vindication for the many controversies he had left in his wake. The saying goes, "You're only as good or bad as your last accomplishment," and Lew needed another successful novel to reinvent himself and elevate his reputation. The next book would have to be bigger and better and attract more readers.

---

2. National Park Service, "11th Regiment, Illinois Cavalry," accessed January 15, 2024, https://www.nps.gov/civilwar/search-battle-units-detail.htm?battleUnitCode=UIL0011RC.

Robert G. Ingersoll

Whether Lew Wallace and Robert Ingersoll knew each other or not is debatable, but they should have; they had a lot in common and crossed paths many times over the years. Like Lew, Ingersoll's birth mother died when he was very young, and later his father remarried. Robert had no formal educational credentials, studied law in Illinois, and, like Abraham Lincoln, became a lawyer. He was a Republican involved in local and national politics. He was a Civil War volunteer officer who recruited and led the Eleventh Illinois Cavalry. He became a much more successful lawyer and speaker than Lew, but later in his career, he became disenchanted with law practice. Robert was a rebel who detested societal shackles and a "free thinker" who debated established contemporary thought, including the Bible and organized religion. He sought the truth based on facts and logic and rejected ideas founded in tradition and faith. Robert loved writers and was a voracious reader who became good friends with the great poet laureate and philosopher Walt Whitman. He even gave Whitman's funeral eulogy.

Lew heard Ingersoll's impressive speech in June of 1875 supporting James G. Blaine at the Republican convention in Cincinnati. Lew was already a successful author; how could he and Ingersoll not have spoken?[1] Ingersoll was a good friend of President Garfield and campaigned for him in his 1880 election campaign. Garfield and Ingersoll had served at Shiloh, the same time and place Lew and Garfield had met. It was

---

1. Morsberger, *Lew Wallace: Militant Romantic*, 298.

common knowledge Lew and Garfield were long-time friends. Ingersoll traveled extensively throughout New Mexico with a group of capitalists, inspecting cattle ranches when Lew was governor.[2] We also know from Sister Blandina Segale that it was local knowledge Ingersoll visited the Palace in Sante Fé on several occasions when Lew was governor and writing the final parts of Ben Hur.

However, Lew and Ingersoll were also very different. Ingersoll's father was a Presbyterian minister who moved his family often during Ingersoll's childhood, slowly progressing from the East Coast to Illinois. He was brought up on the Bible and the *Westminster Shorter Catechism*, and his father relentlessly pushed him to read scripture.[3] The boy was brilliant and started questioning his reading, which frustrated his father. Like Lew's father, Ingersoll's father had many books, and one that stood out was *Fox's Book of Martyrs*, which young Ingersoll found fascinating and terrifying. Like the servant girl had done to Lew in Covington concerning creatures in the forests, this book's stories filled young Ingersoll with terrible fear, and he began having disturbing dreams. Later in life, Ingersoll wrote:

> *The race is under the dominion of Fear—fear of men, ghosts, of hells. I do not fear. I will speak what I think [. . .]. Somebody ought, to tell the truth about the Bible. The preachers dare not, because they would be driven from their pulpits. Professors in colleges dare not, because they would lose their salaries. Politicians dare not. They would be defeated. Editors dare not. They would lose subscribers. Merchants dare not, because they might lose customers. Men of fashion dare not, fearing that they would lose caste. Even clerks dare not, because they might be discharged. And so, I thought I would do it myself.* [4]

Ingersoll insisted he was an agnostic, not an atheist. He claimed he was not an unbeliever but that he simply did not know. Ingersoll wrote,

---

2. Isaac Newton Baker, *An Intimate View of Robert G. Ingersoll*, (Wentworth Press 2022), 68.
3. Ibid., 59.
4. Ibid., 68.

"I wish I did know, but will never pretend, or say, that I do, when I know that I do not. I have the same sources of information, that others have,—all they have—and I know that others do not know. . . . The clergy know that I know that they know they do not know"[5] He did not believe the Bible was the inspired word of God but saw it as a human book, a "very human book." He claimed the Old Testament was merely a history of the Jewish nation and its people. It reflected a history of man's failures and tragedies. It also included the customs and habits of the writers and the people for whom it was written. He contended that the stories were false and impossible and reflected more on man's absurdities than divine inspiration.

As far as the New Testament was concerned, Ingersoll felt Jesus Christ was merely a man and not miraculously conceived. He was born into an ordinary Jewish family and followed his father's trade. That Jesus was unremarkable for much of his life and then walked about performing miracles was very difficult to imagine. Regarding miracles, Robert would say, "They are simply the product of the un-enlightened human imagination, stimulated and perverted by the mistaken zeal of sincerity, or by the designing craft of religious hypocrisy or fanaticism. No miracles are wrought to-day."[6]

Suppose Lew Wallace did meet and discuss these issues with Robert Ingersoll after beginning to write *Ben Hur*. In that case, it's no wonder he might have experienced an epiphany on his train ride to Indianapolis. It might have also disturbed him and could have challenged him while awakening an interest in a subject he had paid little attention. Ingersoll was a polarizing figure who became extremely popular for his blatant disrespect for religion and the Bible, frightening many people from all walks of life. For unbelievers, the thought of a world without organized religion to guide people's ethical and moral compass was a concerning possibility. One can only imagine what the believers thought; we know what Sister Blandina Segale thought.

After the Civil War, people's belief in religion waned. When people live through horrific times, their faith in God is often weakened, and

5. Ibid., 126–27.
6. Ibid., 150–51.

they ask, "How could God allow this to happen?" Robert Ingersoll recognized this and took advantage of the timing to reap fame and fortune via hefty speaking fees. Legend has it that one person in New York paid $3,500 for one front-row ticket to hear him speak (circa 1880). Today, the average Super Bowl ticket is about the same price!

Whether Lew Wallace knew Robert Ingersoll or not, he was writing the right book at the right time and may have sensed the opportunity. People were mentally past the Civil War and tired of doubt, negativity, and cynicism. A religious resurgence was beginning to sprout, and it needed inspiration to bloom. *Ben Hur* provided such an inspiration, and it came at an opportune time written by a great American author.

Epilogue:
Diplomat, Sportsman, Speaker, and Writer

We may as well regard the curtain rung down on this act of my life. I have tried many things in the course of the dream—the law, soldering, politics, authorship, and lastly, diplomacy—and if I may pass judgment upon the success achieved in each, it seems now that when I sit down finally in the old man's gown and slippers, helping the cat to keep the fireplace warm, I shall look back upon Ben-Hur as my best performance, and this mission near the sultan as the next best.

—LEW WALLACE[1]

Upon leaving Santa Fé, Lew and Susan spent the late spring and early summer traveling through Europe on their way to Therapia, a village on the European side of the Bosporus, twelve miles north of the palace of the Sultan of the Ottoman Empire, Abdul Hamid II. The Bosporus was a beautiful and engaging waterway that provided peace and pleasure for Lew and Susan while they awaited the opportunity for Lew to present his credentials to the sultan. The Bosporus connects the Black Sea and the Sea of Marmara, separating the Asian part of Turkey (Anatolia) from the European side. Finally, sometime in August 1881, Lew received word the

---

1. Wallace, An Autobiography, Vol. 2, 969.

sultan would receive him, and Lew invited Susan and US Congressman S.S. Cox to join him. As was usually the case with Lew, it proved to be an unconventional event.

First, they were asked to wait for carriages to take them from the gates to the palace—a leftover custom from the Ottoman Empire days designed to humiliate political guests. They had waited for some time when Lew grew impatient and demanded the carriages come immediately. Astonished and confused, the attending bey escorted the party to a courtyard where carriages had been all along. Then, after meeting with the sultan, Lew asked to shake his hand. The attending bey refused to make the request, and Lew became visibly irritated. The sultan asked what was wrong and demanded to know, and the bey told the sultan what Lew was requesting. The sultan was perplexed as the Turkish people did not do this with each other, let alone with a sultan. Nevertheless, the sultan stepped forward and took Lew's hand. They became great friends, and Sultan Abdul Hamid II often used Lew as a personal advisor.

Lew stayed in Constantinople for four years before returning to Crawfordsville to retire from political and public life to build a study and bury himself in books. Lew also spent many days camping, hunting, and fishing along his favorite little waterway, Sugar Creek, and his property and retreat is now the Crawfordsville Country Club. He came out of retirement to campaign for Benjamin Harrison in the 1888 presidential election. Benjamin was the grandson of William Henry Harrison. Benjamin Harrison defeated Grover Cleveland, the incumbent Democrat, and became the twenty-third president of the United States. Lew also spoke at a US Naval Academy graduation ceremony and to the visitor's board at the West Point Military Academy. He became a member of the board of visitors for both academies, which delighted Lew and must have caused Grant and Henry Halleck to roll over in their graves.

In 1889, a play was written and produced of *Ben Hur*, and it was an overwhelming success in New York and London. In 1890, Lew declined an offer from Benjamin Harrison to become the Minister to Brazil. The *Boyhood of Christ* was published in 1892, and *The Prince of India* in 1893. In 1898, at the age of seventy-one, Lew tried to enlist to fight in the Spanish-American War but was turned away.

On February 15, 1905, Lew passed away at seventy-seven from Atrophic Gastritis, a treatable and curable disease today.[2] It was not the kind of death that Lew would have wanted. One must imagine him dreaming of a hero's death but disappointed by the deadly affliction of a common ailment. Hopefully, he passed dreaming of riding "Old John," his beautiful red sorrel stallion, at the head of his Zouave troops, attacking the enemy at full speed, sword in hand, as rifles crackled and cannons roared behind him—defeating the enemy decisively but struck down by multiple mortal wounds.

Maybe he died hoping a book would be written about him years later to help people in modern times better appreciate him as a significant historical figure, a rare and extraordinary talent, a military hero, and the savior of Washington.

---

2. Atrophic Gastritis is an inflammation of the stomach lining. The inflammation is most often the result of a bacterial infection caused by the H. pylori bacterium. The bacteria disrupt the barrier of mucus that protects your stomach lining from the acidic juices that help with digestion. The infection will gradually destroy the cells in your stomach lining if not treated.

Bibliography

Abbink, Emily *New Mexico's Palace of the Governors, History of an American Treasure,* Museum of New Mexico Press 2007.

Alchetron, "Terry McGovern (boxer)," accessed January 12, 2024, https://alchetron.com/Terry-McGovern-(boxer).

American Battlefield Trust, "Fort Blakley and Spanish Fort," accessed December 30, 2023, https://www.battlefields.org/learn/articles/fort-blakeley-and-spanish-fort.

———, "Richard Montgomery," accessed January 12, 2024, https://www.battlefields.org/learn/biographies/major-general-richard-montgomery.

(The) Army Historical Society, "The Battle of Monocacy 9 July 1864," accessed December 29, 2023, https://armyhistory.org/the-battle-of-monocacy-9-july-1864/.

Baker, Isaac Newton *Intimate View of Robert G. Ingersoll,* Wentworth Press 2022.

Beemer, Charles G. *My Greatest Quarrel with Fortune*, The Kent State University Press, Kent, Ohio 2015.

Biographical Directory of the United States Congress, *"John Test 1781–1849,"* accessed December 30, 2023, https://bioguide.congress.gov/search/bio/T000138.

Blackford, Sheila "Disputed Election of 1876," University of Virginia - Miller Center 2023, accessed: December 30,2023, https://millercenter.org/the-presidency/educational-resources/disputed-election-1876.

Boomhower, Ray E. *The Sword & the Pen, A Life of Lew Wallace*, Indiana Historical Society Press 2005.

———. "Lew Wallace," Indiana Historical Society, accessed October 22, 2023, https://secure.in.gov/history/about-indiana-history-and-trivia/annual-commemorations/civil-war-150th/hoosier-voices-now/lew-wallace/.

Boze, Bell *The Illustrated Life and Times of Billy the Kid, Second Edition*, Tri Star Boze Productions, Inc. 1996.

Buley, R.C. "Indiana in the Mexican War," Indiana University Press, Ind. Magazine of History, September 1919.

Chávez, Thomas E. *An Illustrated History of New Mexico* (Reprint Edition), University of New Mexico 2002.

Chipman, N.P. *The Tragedy of Andersonville*, Self Published 1911.

Creason, Carl C. "Puritan Hypocrisy and Conservative Catholicity," The University of Louisville, May 2016, accessed October 9, 2023, https://ir.library.louisville.edu/etd/2430/.

Cunningham, Edward *Shiloh and the Western Campaign of 1862*, Savas Beati, 2009.

Davis, David Ex Parte Milligan, 71 U.S. 2 (1866).

eyeXam Silicon Valley, accessed December 28, 2023, https:eyeexam.com/6-rare-unique-eye-colors/.

(The) Economic Historian, "Panic of 1837," accessed December 30,2023, https://economic-historian.com/2020/07/panic-of-1837/.

———, "Panic of 1857," accessed December 30,2023, https://economic-historian.com/2020/07/panic-of-1857/.

Editors "The Assassins and the Jurisdiction of Military Tribunals," The New York Times, May 16, 1865, accessed October 23, 2023, https://www.nytimes.com/1865/05/16/archives/the-assassins-and-the-jurisdiction-of-military-tribunals.html.

Editors "Cinco de Mayo," History.com, April 29, 2022, accessed October 23.2023, https://www.history.com/topics/holidays/cinco-de-mayo.

Editors Civil War Talk, "Major General Lew Wallace (USA)," May 11, 2017, accessed December 30, 2023, https://civilwartalk.com/threads/major-general-lew-wallace-usa.134443/.

Editors Goodreads, "Lew Wallace Quotes," accessed October 23, 2023, https://www.goodreads.com/quotes/570224-youth-is-but-the-painted-shell-within-which-continually-growing.

Editors "Harpers Ferry Raid," Britannica Online Encyclopedia October 9, 2020, accessed January 15, 2024, https://www.britannica.com/event/Harpers-Ferry-Raid.

Editors "Henry W. Halleck," Britannica Online Encyclopedia, November 7, 2021, accessed October 23, 2023, https://www.britannica.com/biography/henry-w-halleck.

Editors "William Henry Harrison," History.com, August 21, 2018, accessed: October 23, 2023, https://www.history.com/topics/us-presidents/william-henry-harrison.

Editors "The Rebel Assassins," The New York Times Archives, August 22, 1865, accessed: October 23, 2023, https://www.nytimes.com/1865/08/22/archives/the-rebel-assassins-trial-of-henry-wirz-the-andersonville.html.

Editors, *Trial of the Assassins at Washington*, T.B. Peterson & Brothers, Philadelphia, PA, 1865, "Trial of the Assassins at Washington," accessed December 29, 2023, https://archive.org/details/trialofallegedas00unit/page/n5/mode/2up.

Editors "Ulysses S. Grant's Lifelong Struggle with Alcohol," Historynet.com, June 12, 2006, accessed October 23, 2023, https://www.historynet.com/ulysses-s-grants-lifelong-struggle-with-alcohol/.

Eicher John H. & David J. *Civil War High Commands,* Stanford University Press 2001.

Farber, Zac, "Politics of the Past: 'Grave Doubt' couldn't stop hanging," Minnesota Lawyer, February 28, 2017, accessed October 23, 2023, https://minnlawyer.com/2017/02/28/politics-of-the-past-grave-doubts-couldnt-stop-hanging/.

Farrelly, Maura Jane *Anti-Catholicism in America 1620-1860*, Cambridge University Press 2018.

Fireside, Bryna J. *The Mary Surratt "Lincoln Assassination Trial,"* Enslow Publishers Inc. 2001.

Fisher, Louis "Military Tribunals: Historical Patterns and Lessons," The Library of Congress, July 9, 2004.

Foreign Service Institute United States Department of State, Office of the Historian, "French Intervention in Mexico and the American Civil War, 1862–1867," accessed December 30, 2023, https://history.state.gov/milestones/1861-1865/french-intervention.

Futch, Ovid L. *History of Andersonville Prison* (Revised Edition), University Press of Florida, 1999.

General Lew Wallace Study & Museum, "Diplomat," https://www.ben-hur.com/meet-lew-wallace/diplomat/, (accessed January 13, 2024).

———, "Lew Wallace in Mexico,", accessed January 12, 2024, https://www.ben-hur.com/lew-wallace-in-mexico/.

Getchell, Kevin *Scapegoat of Shiloh*, McFarland & Company, Inc. 2013.

Goodreads, "Lew Wallace Quotes", https://www.goodreads.com/quotes/570224-youth-is-but-the-painted-shell-within-which-continually-growing, (accessed: October 23, 2023).

Grant, Ulysses S. *Personal Memoirs of Ulysses S. Grant, Vol. 1*, Charles L. Webster & Company 1885.

———. *Personal Memoirs of Ulysses S. Grant, Vol. 2*, Charles L. Webster & Company 1886.

Hall, Michael *The Road to Washington: Henry S. Lane*, Montgomery County Historical Society 1990.

Helling, William R. *Images of America, Crawfordsville,* Arcadia Publishing 2011.

Indiana Department of Administration, "Ashbel P. Willard", accessed December 30,2023, https://www.in.gov/idoa/statehouse/notable-hoosiers-in-sculpture/ashbel-parsons-willard/.

Indiana Governor History, "Henry Smith Lane," accessed December 30, 2023, https://www.in.gov/governorhistory/by-year/henry-smith-lane/.

Indiana Historical Bureau, "Indiana Governor Oliver Perry Morton," https://www.in.gov/history/about-indiana-history-and-trivia/governors-portraits/list-of-governors/indiana-governor-oliver-perry-morton-1823-1877/, (accessed: January 11, 2024).

Indy., "Billy the Kid was a famous Old West outlaw, But Indiana ties shaped his roots and fate," accessed January 17, 2024, https://www.indystar.com/story/entertainment/arts/2023/11/01/billy-the-kid-old-west-outlaw-indianapolis-anderson-indiana-ties/70662161007/.

Jackson, Stephen T. "In History: Was Billy the Kid from Anderson," Herald Bulletin, Anderson, Indiana, June 19, 2014, accessed October 23, 2023, https://www.heraldbulletin.com/archives/in-history-was-billy-the-kid-from-anderson/article_b6579798-ac8e-553b-a204-37a35ba9fe80.html.

Jacobs, William R. "William H. Prescot, American historian," Britanica Online Encyclopedia, accessed: January 12, 2024, https://www.britannica.com/biography/William-H-Prescott.

Joseph Holt Home, "Joseph Holt," accessed January 12, 2024 https://josephholthome.com/history/.

JSTOR, "The Catholic Press, the Bible, and Protestant Responsibility for the Civil War," accessed January 15, 2024, https://www.jstor.org/stable/26381449.

Kantor, MacKinlay *Andersonville*, The World Publishing Company 1955.

Klement, Frank L. *Dark Lanterns: Secret Political Societies*, Louisiana State University Press 1984.

LaForce, Cpt. Glen W. "The Trial of Major Henry Wirz, A National Disgrace," The Army Lawyer, June 1988.

Larson, Orvin Prentiss, *American Infidel, Robert G. Ingersoll a Biography,* Hassell Street Press 1993.

Lewis, James "Black Hawk War," Britannica Online Encyclopedia, accessed December 30, 2023, https://www.britannica.com/event/Black-Hawk-War.

Library of Congress, "*Baltimore American*, April 21, 1865," accessed January 15, 2024, https://www.loc.gov/item/scsm001197/.

———, "*Baltimore American*, April 25th, 1865," accessed January 15, 2024, https://www.loc.gov/item/scsm001212/.

———, "New York Times Archives, May 16, 1865," accessed: September 2, 2023, https://www.loc.gov/item/scsm001326/.

Lieber, Francis LL.D. "United States Government Field Instructions Manual," U.S. Govt., General Order No. 100, AJO 1863.

Lincoln Conspirators.com, "May 6, 1865", accessed December 30,2023, https://lincoln conspirators.com/the-trial/may-6-1865/.

Long, Lessel *Twelve Months in Andersonville,* Big Byte Books 2015 (Orig. publ. 1886).

McElroy, Joh, *Andersonville, A Story of Rebel Prisons,* The Project Ebook of Andersonville, Vol. 1, 116, 1879.

Miller, Michael, "'Assassins!': A Confederate spy was accused of helping kill Abraham Lincoln. Then he vanished.", Washington Post, April 13, 2017, accessed: December30,2023, https://www.washingtonpost.com/news/retropolis/wp/2017/04/13/assassins-a-confederate-spy-was-accused-of-helping-kill-abraham-lincoln-then-he-vanished/.

Moore, Guy W. *The Case of Mrs. Surratt,* University of Oklahoma Press, Norman 1954.

Morseberger, Robert & Katherine *Lew Wallace: Militant Romantic,* McGraw-Hill Book Company 1980.

Mortenson, Christopher R. *Politician in Uniform, General Lew Wallace and the Civil War,* Norman, OK, University of Oklahoma Press 2019.

National Park Service, "11th Regiment, Illinois Cavalry," accessed January 15, 2024, https://www.nps.gov/civilwar/search-battle-units-detail.htm?battle UnitCode=UIL0011RC.

National Park Service, "Myth: Grant Stopped the Prisoner Exchange," accessed: January 1, 2024, https://www.nps.gov/ande/learn/historyculture/grant-and-the-prisoner-exchange.htm.

National Portrait Gallery, Smithsonian, "The Battle of Shiloh", April 6-7, 1862, accessed December 29, 2023, https://npg.si.edu/blog/battle-shiloh-april-6-7-1862.

Newspapers.com by Ancestry, "O'Crowley, Hawkeye and Weichmann," accessed: January 12, 2024, https://www.newspapers.com/article/anderson-daily-bulletin-ocrowley-hawkey/4718454/.

New York Times Archives, accessed: September 2, 2023, https://archive.nytimes.com/www.nytimes.com/ref/membercenter/nytarchive.html.

Nolan, Frederick *The Lincoln War: A Documentary History,* Norman, OK, University of Oklahoma Press 1992.

———. *The West of Billy the Kid,* Norman, OK, University of Oklahoma Press 1998.

———. *The Billy the Kid Reader,* Norman, OK, University of Oklahoma Press 2007.

O'Brien, David, *Public Catholicism,* Macmillan Publishing Company 1989.

Oliace, Beth "Blaze burns away county records", *The Herald Bulletin,* Anderson, Indiana, December 22, 2012, accessed October 21, 2023, https://www.heraldbulletin.com/community/blaze-burns-away-county-records/article_64141797-94b6-5565-a0c9-570bf2bedff6.html.

———, "Louis Weichmann, Anderson's Connection to the Lincoln Assassination," The Herald Bulletin, Anderson, Indiana, February 22, 2014, accessed October 21, 2023, https://www.heraldbulletin.com/community/history-louis-weichmann-andersons-connection-to-the-lincoln-assassination/article_8c59e942-f5a4-58f1-9671-98acd6e6c1db.html.

Online Books: Official Records, Union and confederate Reports (Pages 134-135) The War of the Rebellion: A compilation of the Official Records of the Union and Confederate Armies, by the United States War Department, 1880, accessed: December, 12, 2023, https://civilwarindex.com/WV/skirmish_on_pattersons_creek.html.

Page, James Madison *The True Story of Andersonville Prison,* (Originally published by The Neale Publishing Company 1908), Forgotten Books, 2015.

Pitman, Benn *The Assassination of President Lincoln,* Forgotten Books 2017.

Quint, Ryan T. *Determined to Stand and Fight: The Battle of Monocacy July 9, 1864*, Civil War Series, El Dorado Hills, CA: Savas Beatie 2017.

Ransom, John L. *Andersonville Diary*, Big Byte Books 2016.

Segale, Sister Blandina *At the End of the Santa Fé Trail*, Pathfinder Books 2013.

Smith, Timothy B. "Why Lew Was Late," Civil War Times, November 14, 2021, accessed October 23, 2023, https://www.historynet.com/why-lew-was-late.htm.

Smith, Justin H. *The Annexation of Texas*, (Orig. publ. University of Virginia 1941), Barnes & Noble 2022.

Spacebattles, "For a Sword, Sarah Hutchins", accessed: December 30, 2023, https://forums. spacebattles.com/threads/all-for-a-sword-the-military-trial-of-sarah-hutchins-for -treason.823730/.

Stephens, Gail *Shadow of Shiloh, Major General Lew Wallace in the Civil War,* Indiana Historical Society Press, Indianapolis 2010.

Thoreau, Henry *David Civil Disobedience: Complete Texts and Introduction, Historical Contexts, Critical Essays*, Houghton Mifflin, 2000.

Tikkanen, Amy, "Andersonville", Britanica Online Encyclopedia, accessed: 01-03-2024, https:// www.britannica.com/place/Andersonville-Georgia.

Tikkanen, Amy, "Battle of Buena Vista," Britanica Online Encyclopedia, accessed January 2, 2024, https://www.britannica.com/event/Battle-of-Buena-Vista.

Trial of the Assassins At Washington, (T.B. Peterson & Brothers, Philadelphia, PA, 1865), accessed January 15,2024, https://archive.org/details/trialofallegedas00unit/page/n5/ mode/2up.

Trinidad, Elizabeth Steger *Mary Surratt, An American Tragedy,* Pelican Publishing Company 1996.

Uenuma, Francine "During the Mexican-American War, Irish-Americans Fought for Mexico in the 'Saint Patrick's Battalion," Smithsonianmag.com, March 15, 2019, accessed 23, 2023. https://www.smithsonianmag.com/history/mexican-american-war-irish-immigrants deserted-us-army-fight-against-america-180971713/.

United States Senate, "Presidential Succession Act." Accessed January 17, 2024, https://www. senate.gov/about/officers-staff/president-pro-tempore/presidential-succession-act.htm.

United States War Department. *The War of the Rebellion: a Compilation of the Official Records of the Union and Confederate Armies.* Series 1, 53 vols. Secretary of War, et al. Washington, D.C.: Government Printing Office, 1880-1901.

University of Missouri-K.C. School of Law. "The Execution of Captain Henry Wirz," accessed January 17, 2024, http://law2.umkc.edu/Faculty/projects/FTrials/Wirz/executin.htm.

Utley, Robert M. "Victorio's War," Historynet, June 2, 2022, accessed October 23, 2023, https://www.historynet.com/Victorios-war/.

Utley, Robert M. *Billy the Kid, a Short and Violent Life,* University of Nebraska Press 1989.

Wallace, Lew Ben *Hur, A Tale of the Christ,* Wadsworth Editions Limited, 1996.

———. *An Autobiography, Vol. 1,* Forgotten Books 2015.

———. *An Autobiography, Vol. 2,* Forgotten Books 2015.

———. *The Fair God,* Houghton, Mifflin & Company, 1885 (Orig. publ. 1873).

Walsh, Richard *Maryland, A History 1632-1974,* Baltimore, Maryland Historical Society 1974.

Weddle, Jerry "Antrim is My Stepfather's Name," The Arizona Historical Society 1993.

Weichmann, Louis J. *A True History of the Assassination of Abraham Lincoln,* Alfred A Knopf 1975.

Wheeler, Linda, The Washington Post, July 7, 2015, "President Johnson claimed to not have seen a clemency petition for Mary Surratt," accessed: 12-29-2023, https://www. washingtonpost.com/news/house-divided/wp/2015/07/07/president-johnson-claimed-to -not-have-seen-a-clemency-petition-for-mary-surratt/.

White House, The "Ulysses S. Grant, The 18th President of the United States," accessed September 2, 2023, https://www.whitehouse.gov/about-the-white-house/presidents/ulysses-s-grant/.

———, The "William Henry Harrison, The 9th President of the United States," accessed December 30,2023, https://www.whitehouse.gov/about-the-white-house/presidents/william-henry-harrison/.

———, The "Zachary Taylor, The 12th President of the United States," accessed: January 12, 2024, https://www.whitehouse.gov/about-the-white-house/presidents/zachary-taylor/.

———, The "John Tyler, The 10th President of the United States", accessed: January 12, 2024, https://www.whitehouse.gov/about-the-white-house/presidents/john-tyler/.

Wilson, James Harrison *The Life of John A. Rawlins*, Independently Published, 2016 (Orig. publ 1916).

Woollen, William Wesley *Biographical and Historical Sketches of Early Indiana*, Ayer Publishing 1975.

WomensHistory.org., "The First Woman Executed by the US Government," accessed December 29,2023, https://www.womenshistory.org/articles/first-woman-executed-us-government.

Zanca, Kenneth J. *The Catholics and Mrs. Marry Surratt*, University Press of America 2008.

Zeidan, Adam "Invasion and War," Britannica Online Encyclopedia, (accessed: September 2, 2023, https://www.britanica.com/event/Mexican-American/War/Invasion-and-war.

About the Author

MICHAEL E. FOX was raised in Crawfordsville, Indiana. During childhood, he had contacts with people who knew and remembered the great American author Lew Wallace. Lew Wallace wrote seven of his eight parts of Ben Hur in Crawfordsville, and Lew's study/museum is located there. Mr. Fox has been interested in 19th-century history and has read extensive books and articles concerning this period, notably Lew Wallace. In 1976, he graduated from Purdue University and was recruited to work at the R.R. Donnelley & Sons' Crawfordsville book printing plant. As a first-line supervisor and quality control expert, he would proofread, sometimes wholly read, and examine nearly every type of book printed. He also worked closely with quality experts from major domestic and international publishers.

In 1981 he went to work for the Eastman Kodak Company in Rochester, New York, before moving to high-tech equipment and software manufacturing. In 1991, he graduated from night Law School and became a licensed attorney. In 2005, he became President of Screen GP Americas, a manufacturer of high-speed, high-resolution ink-jet printing equipment. He sold the first machine in North and South America. Mr. Fox is considered a pioneer in modern-day printing and publishing technology. In 2012, he earned his Master of Law (LLM) with Honors. In 2020, Mr. Fox retired from Screen, moved to Southern California, and began pursuing his lifetime passion of publishing a book about 19th-century history and Lew Wallace.

www.ingramcontent.com/pod-product-compliance
Lightning Source LLC
Chambersburg PA
CBHW021141090426
42740CB00008B/878